Henry Spencer Kenrick Bellairs, Laxman Y. Ashkedar

A Grammar of the Marathi Language

Henry Spencer Kenrick Bellairs, Laxman Y. Ashkedar

A Grammar of the Marathi Language

ISBN/EAN: 9783743393523

Manufactured in Europe, USA, Canada, Australia, Japa

Cover: Foto ©Thomas Meinert / pixelio.de

Manufactured and distributed by brebook publishing software (www.brebook.com)

Henry Spencer Kenrick Bellairs, Laxman Y. Ashkedar

A Grammar of the Marathi Language

A GRAMMAR

OF THE

MARATHI LANGUAGE,

BY

H. S. K. BELLAIRS, M.A. (OXFORD),

AND

LAXMAN Y. ASKHEDKAR, B.A. (BOMBAY).

Bombay:

PRINTED AT THE
EDUCATION SOCIETY'S PRESS, BYCULLA.

1868.

Dedication.

TO

Sir ALEXANDER GRANT, Baronet,

&c. &c. &c.

Sir,

We dedicate this book to you, hoping that it may prove a help to the cause in which you have taken so much interest, and for which you have done so much.

Your obedient Servants,

H. S. K. BELLAIRS,

LAXMAN Y. ASKHEDKAR.

Belgaum, 1868.

PREFACE.

To gain a critical and accurate knowledge of the Marathi language has, up to the present time, been almost impossible for Europeans.

Dadoba Pandurang's and Krishna Shastri Godabola's Marathi Grammars, invaluable as they are, present insurmountable difficulties to any but very advanced scholars. Dr. Stevenson's Grammar is worse than useless. Its errors are too numerous to be dealt with here *seriatim*. Amongst the more striking may be mentioned wrong system of declensions; absurd rules and intricacies with regard to genders, numbers, and cases; endless errors as to verbs, and spelling.

The truth of these assertions may be proved by any student of Marathi by a comparison of of Dr. Stevenson's Grammar with that of Mr. Dadoba, Mr. Godabola, or our own. We have generally followed the system pursued by Mr. Benfey in his Sanscrit Grammar; and we have freely made use of Mr. Dadoba's, Mr. Godabola's, and Professor Wilson's works.

We acknowledge with gratitude the kindness shown to us by Professor Mahadeva Govind Ranade, who has given us his advice in our difficulties.

CONTENTS.

	PAGE
Alphabet	1
Phonetic Rules	3
The Parts of Speech	4
Substantives	5
Declensions, 1st	8
,, 2nd	10
,, 3rd	13
,, 4th	14
,, 5th	15
,, 6th	15
,, 7th	16
Pronouns	17
Adjectives	26
Numerals	27
Verbs	31
Adverbs	63
Particles	64
Compounds	64
Verb Constructions	66
Syntax	68
Prosody	75
Appendix	82

MARÂTHI GRAMMAR.

PART I.

The Marâthi Alphabet consists of forty-seven letters. Of these fourteen are vowels and thirty-three consonants.

Sounds.	Hard or surd.		Soft or sonant.							
Gutturals ..	क	ख	..	ग	घ	ङ	ह	अ	आ	..	..
Palatals	च	छ	श	ज	झ	ञ	य	इ	ई	ए	ऐ
Cerebrals ..	ट	ठ	ष	ड	ढ	ण	र	ऋ	ॠ	..	..
Dentals	त	थ	स	द	ध	न	ल	ऌ	ॡ	..	..
Labials	प	फ	..	ब	भ	म	व	उ	ऊ	ओ	औ

1. Besides these there is a nasal, called Anuswâra, denoted by a dot above the letter after which it is to be pronounced; ex., राजांत Râjânt.

2. An aspirate, called Visarga, denoted by two dots placed one above the other : ex., प्रातःकाळ Prâtahkâl.

N.B. ऌ *li* is not found in Sanscrit Grammars. क्ष *ksha*, compounded of क and ष, and ज्ञ *jnya*, compounded of ज and ञ, are in common use as simple letters. ळ *lla* is often used in Marâthi, being frequently substituted for the Sanscrit ल.

1 M G

The letters are pronounced as follows:—

अ	a	like	a	in	arena.
आ	â	,,	a	,,	far
इ	i	,,	i	,,	film.
ई	î	,,	ee	,,	feet.
उ	u	,,	u	,,	full.
ऊ	û	,,	oo	,,	root.
ऋ	ri	,,	ri	,,	rid.
ॠ	rî	,,	rea	,,	read.
ऌ	li	,,	li	,,	lick.
ॡ	lî	,,	lea	,,	lead.
ए	e	,,	a	,,	fate.
ऐ	ai	,,	ai	,,	mai (Italian).
ओ	o	,,	o	,,	note.
औ	ou	,,	ow	,,	vow.

Anusvâra (ं) like *ng* in king.

Visarga (:) ha, like *ha* in Minne*ha*ha.

क	ka	like *cu*	in cup		ड	ḍa	like *du*	in dun
ख	kha	,, *kh*	,, khan		ढ	ḍha	,, *dh*	,, adhesion
ग	ga	,, *gu*	,, gull		ण	ṇa	,, *nn*	,, conned
घ	gha	,, *gh*	,, Afghan		त	ta	,, *tu*	,, tub
ङ	ng	,, *ng*	,, sung		थ	tha	,, *thu*	,, thunder
च	cha	,, *chu*	,, church		द	da	,, *du*	,, dunce
छ	chha	,, *chh*	,, chink		ध	dha	,, *dh*	,, sandhill
ज	ja	,, *ju*	,, jut		न	na	,, *nu*	,, nut
झ	za	,, *dz*	,, adze		प	pa	,, *pu*	,, pup
ञ	ṇa	,, *n*	,, singe		फ	pha	,, *ph*	,, shepherd
ट	ṭa	,, *to*	,, atom		ब	ba	,, *bu*	,, but
ठ	ṭha	,, *t-h*	,, at-home		भ	bha	,, *bh*	,, abhor

म	ma	like *mu* in mummy	श	sha	like *shu* in shut
य	ya	„ *you* „ young	ष	*sha*	„ *shu* „ shun
र	ra	„ *ru* „ run	स	sa	„ *su* „ subtle
ल	la	„ *lu* „ lung	ह	ha	„ *hu* „ hut
व	va	„ *wo* „ won	ळ	lla	„ *ll* „ hall

N.B.—Vowels and diphthongs are joined to consonants as follows:—

क ka, का kâ, कि ki, की kî, कु ku, कू kû, कृ kri,
कॄ krî, कॢ kli, कॣ klî, के ke, कै kaî, को ko, कौ kow,
कं kam, कः kaha.

Out of the vowels given above the following are diphthongs:—ए, ऐ, ओ, औ.

In Marâṭhi when two or more consonants come together, they may be combined either by placing the one consonant under the other, or by omitting the transverse line of all the consonants except the last: ex., स्वच्छ Svachchha; this word is composed of the following letters:—स् s, व् v, च् ch, छ् chh.

N.B.—Every consonant in Marâthi contains the vowel अ a (unless it has the विराम Virâma mark (्) placed under it), and this vowel has a sound similar to that of either of the *a's* in arena. Thus न is not pronounced like the English *n*, but like the *na* at the end of the word are*na*.

PHONETIC RULES.

I. Homogeneous vowels meeting together at the end and the beginning either of separate words or parts of a compound, combine into one long homogeneous vowel: ex.—

अ or आ + अ or आ = आ   स्वर्ग + आणि = स्वर्गाणि
इ or ई + इ or ई = ई   कवि + ईश्वर = कवीश्वर
उ or ऊ + उ or ऊ = ऊ   भानु + उदय = भानूदय
ऋ or ॠ + ऋ or ॠ = ॠ   पितृ + ऋण = पितॄण

II. When अ or आ at the end of a word or part of a compound meets other vowels of the beginning of other words, changes take place as follows :—

अ or आ + इ i or ई î = ए ex. देव + ईश्वर = देवेश्वर.
अ or आ + उ u or ऊ û = ओ ex. सूर्य + उदय = सूर्योदय.
अ or आ + ऋ ri or ॠ rî = अर् ex. ब्रह्म + ऋषि = ब्रह्मर्षि.
अ or आ + ए e or ऐ ai = ऐ ex. एक + एक = ऐकैक.
अ or आ + ओ o or औ ow = औ ex. वन + औषध = वनौषध.

III. When a word, or the first part of a compound, ends in इ i or ई î, उ u or ऊ û, ऋ ri or ॠ rî ऌ li or ॡ lî, and the following begins with a heterogeneous vowel or a diphthong, इ i and ई î are changed to य्, उ u and ऊ û to व्, ऋ and ॠ to र्, and ऌ and ॡ to ल्.

IV. A final क् k, त् t, त् t, प् p followed by a sonant letter is changed to the corresponding sonant: namely, ग् g, ड् ḍ, द् d, ब् b.

PARTS OF SPEECH,

OR

CLASSES OF WORDS.

The words of the Marâthi language may be arranged in three classes.—viz, Nouns, Verbs, and Particles.

Nouns are either substantives, adjectives, or adverbs. (Pronouns, *i. e.* words standing for nouns, are of three kinds; substantival, adjectival, and adverbial.) Particles are either postpositions or conjunctions.

Interjections are extra-grammatical words.

SUBSTANTIVES.

A substantive is the name of a distinct and independent existence, whether real or ideal.

Substantives are proper names, or common nouns, or abstract nouns.

Substantives in Marâthi are inflected; and they have two numbers, singular and plural.

By inflection the Marâthi language indicates eight general relations, and accordingly has eight cases, viz:—Nominative, Accusative, Instrumental, Dative, Ablative, Genitive, Locative, and Vocative, which are distinguished by terminations or postpositions.

Gender.

There are but very few rules of use in finding the genders of Marâthi Nouns; the student must generally trust to the dictionary.

Names and appellations of males are masculine· The following also are masculine :—Names of mountains, seas, days, planets, winds, life, affections of the mind and names of large objects as opposed to small of the same class, which are feminine. Exc.:—

दर्या, Daryâ (*f.*) sea. अरुन्धती Arundhatî (*f.*). हवा Havâ (*f.*) air. दया Dayâ (*f.*) pity. कृपा Kripâ (*f.*) favour. करुणा Karunâ (*f.*) pity. माया Mâyâ (*f.*) love.

ममता Mamatâ (f.) love.	इच्छा Ichchhâ (f.) desire.
ईर्षा Irshâ (f.) emulation.	क्षमा Kshamâ (f.) pardon.
शंका Shankâ (f.) doubt.	वासना Vâsanâ (f.) inclination.
वांछा Vânchhâ (f.) desire.	अदावत Adâvat (f.) enmity.

Feminine.

Names and appellations of females are feminine. Nouns ending in इ i and ई î (excepting names and appellations of men) are generally feminine. (N.B.—For this rule it is not necessary that the letters इ i or ई î should be written at the end of a word; ex. काठी, the last syllable of which really contains the consonant ठ् and the vowel ई î, which are amalgamated into ठी).

Exc. :—

अग्नि Agni (m.) fire. पक्षी Pakshî (m.) a bird. पाणि Pâni (m.) Palm of the hand. पाणी Pânî (n.) water. बलि Bali (m.) an offering.

And a few other Sanskrit words.

The termination ईण îna, ऊक nûka, and वळ vala are generally feminine.

Nouns having the anuswâra on the last letter are always neuter.

Nouns ending in पण pana and त्व tva are always neuter.

Number.

Masc. nouns ending in the sing. in अ, इ, ऊ, ओ retain the same form in the plural.

Fem. ,, ,, आ

Masc. nouns ending in the sing. in आ change to ए in the plural.
Fem. ,, ,, अ ,, ई or आ ,,
,, ,, ,, ई ,, या ,, ,,
,, ,, ,, ओ ,, आ ,, ,,
Neut. ,, ,, अ ऊ } ,, एं ,, ,,
,, ,, ,, ,, ,, ,,
,, ,, ,, ई ,, यें ,, ,,
,, ,, ,, एं ,, ई ,, ,,

Ex. :—   Sing.   Plu.
         घोडा.   घोडे.
         भिंत, लात.   भिंती, लाता.
         काठी.   काठया.
         बायको   बायका.
         पान, लेंकरूं.   पानें लेंकरें.
         मोतीं.   मोत्यें.
         तळें.   तळीं.

In Marâthi there are seven declensions.

The following table exhibits all the case-endings of the seven declensions:—

Case.	Singular.	Plural.
Accusative	ला. स. तें.	नां. ला. स. तें.
Instrumental ..	नें. एं. शीं.	नीं. हीं. ई. शीं.
Dative	ला. स. तें. अर्थ.	नां. स. तें. अर्थ.
Ablative	ऊन. हून. तून.	ऊन. हून. तून.
Genitive	चा. ची. चें.	चा. ची. चें.
Locative	त. ई आं.	त. इं. आं.

First Declension.

The first declension comprises those nouns whose crude form can take inflections. It contains honorific nouns ending in आ â; proper nouns ending in a long vowel; nouns ending in ओ o, nouns containing more than one letter and ending in ई î. (Exc. Nouns expressing a profession generally belong to the 7th declension. Ex. न्हावी). Some masculine and feminine nouns ending in ऊ û, and all nouns containing one letter only.

राजा (*m.*) a king.

Case.	Sing.	Plu.
Nom.	राजा	राजे
Acc.	राजास-ला-तें	राजांस-ला-तें-नां
Inst.	राजानें-शीं	राजानीं-शीं-हीं
Dat.	राजास-ला-तें	राजांस-ला-नां
Abl.	राजापासून-हून	राजांपासून-हून
Gen.	राजाचा-ची-चें	राजांचा-ची-चें
Loc.	राजांत	राजांत
Voc.	राजा	राजांनो

दादा (*m.*) Dâdâ.

Case.	Sing.	Plu.
Nom.	दादा	दादा
Acc.	दादास-ला-तें	दादांस-ला-तें-नां
Inst.	दादानें-शीं	दादानीं-हीं-शीं
Dat.	दादास-ला-तें	दादांस-ला-नां
Abl.	दादापासून-हून	दादांपासून-हून
Gen.	दादाचा-चो-चें	दादांचा-ची-चें
Loc.	दादांत	दादांत
Voc.	दादा	दादांनो

बायको (*f.*) a woman.

Case.	Sing.	Plur.
Nom.	बायको	बायका
Acc.	बायकोला-स-तें	बायकांना-ला-स
Inst.	बायकोनें-शीं	बायकानीं-हीं-शीं
Dat.	बायकोस-ला-तें	बायकांला-ना-स
Abl.	बायकाहून-पासून	बायकाहून-पासून
Gen.	बाहकोचा-ची-चें	बायकांचा-ची-चें
Loc.	बायकोंन	बायकांत
Voc.	बायको	बायकांनों

दासी (*f.*) a maid-servant.

Case.	Sing.	Plu.
Nom.	दासी	दासी
Acc.	दासीस-ला-तें	दासींना-ला-तें
Inst.	दासीनें-शीं	दासोंनीं-हीं-शीं
Dat.	दासीस-ला-तें	दासींना-ला-तें
Abl.	दासीहून-पासून	दासींहून-पासून
Gen.	दासीचा-ची-चें	दासींचा-ची-चें
Loc.	दासींत	दासींत
Voc.	दासी	दासींनों

चाकू (*m.*) a pen-knife.

Case.	Sing.	Plu.
Nom.	चाकू.	चाकू.
Acc.	चाकूस-ला-तें	चाकूंस-ला-तें.
Inst.	चाकूनें-शीं.	चाकूंनीं-हीं-शीं
Dat.	चाकूस-ला-तें.	चाकूंस-ला-तें.
Abl.	चाकूपासून-हून	चाकूंपासून-हून.
Gen.	चाकूचा-ची-चें.	चाकूंचा-ची-चें
Loc.	चाकूंत.	चाकूंत.
Voc.	चाकू.	चाकूंनों.

वधू (*f.*) a bride.

Case.	Sing.	Plu.
Nom.	वधू	वधू
Acc.	वधूस-ला-तें	वधूंना-ला-तें
Inst.	वधूनें-शीं	वधूंनीं-हीं-शीं
Dat.	वधूस-ला-तें	वधूंना-ला-तें
Abl.	वधूहून-पासून	वधूंहून-पासून
Gen.	वधूचा-ची-चें	वधूंचा-ची-चें
Loc.	वधूंन	वधूंत
Voc.	वधू	वधूंनों

ऊ (*f.*) a louse.

Case.	Sing.	Plu.
Nom.	ऊ	उवा
Acc.	ऊस-ला-तें	उवांना-ला-तें
Inst.	ऊनें-शीं	उवांनीं-हीं-शीं
Dat.	ऊस-ला-तें	उवांना-ला-तें
Abl.	ऊहून-पासून	उवांइन-पासून
Gen.	ऊचा-ची-चें	उवांचा-ची-चें
Loc.	ऊंत	उवांत
Voc.	ऊ	उवांनों

Second Declension.

The second declension comprises those nouns whose crude forms must be modified by lengthening the last vowel before they can be inflected. It contains masculine nouns ending in अ a, इ i, and उ u, and some feminine nouns in इ i, and उ u, and neuter nouns in अ a.

देव (m.) God.

Case.	Sing.	Plu.
Nom.	देव	देव
Acc.	देवास-ला-तें	देवांना-स-ला-तें
Inst.	देवानें-शीं	देवांनीं-हीं-शीं
Dat.	देवास-ला-तें	देवांना-ला-तें
Abl.	देवापासून-हून	देवांपासून-हून
Gen.	देवाचा-ची-चें	देवांचा-ची-चें
Loc.	देवांत	देवांन
Voc.	देवा	देवांनों

कवि (m.) a poet.

Case.	Sing.	Plu.
Nom.	कवि	कवि
Acc.	कवीस-ला-तें	कवींस-ला-तें-नां
Inst.	कवीनें-शीं	कवींनीं-शीं
Dat.	कवीला-स-तें	कवींला-स-तें-नां
Abl.	कवीपासून-हून	कवींपासून-हून
Gen.	कवीचा-ची-चें	कवींचा-ची-चें
Loc.	कवींत	कवींत
Voc.	कवो	कवींनों

गुरु (m.) a preceptor.

Case.	Sing.	Plu.
Nom.	गुरु	गुरु
Acc.	गुरुस-ला-तें	गुरुंना-ला-तें
Inst.	गुरुनें-शीं	गुरुंनीं-हीं-शीं
Dat.	गुरुस-ला-तें	गुरुंना-ला-तें
Abl.	गुरुपासून-हून	गुरुंपासून-हून
Gen.	गुरुचा-ची-चें	गुरुंचा-ची-चें
Loc.	गुरुंत	गुरुंत
Voc.	गुरु	गुरुंनों

रुचि (*f.*) taste.

Case.	Sing.	Plu.
Nom.	रुचि	रुचि
Acc.	रुचीस-ला-तें	रुचींस-ला-तें-ना
Inst.	रुचीनें-शीं	रुचीनीं-हीं-शीं
Dat.	रुचीस-ला-तें	रुचींस-ला-तें-ना
Abl.	रुचीपासून-हून	रुचींपासून-हून
Gen.	रुचीचा-ची-चें	रुचींचा-ची-चें
Loc.	रुचींत	रुचींत
Voc.	रुची	रुचींनो

रेणु (*f.*) an atom.

Case.	Sing.	Plu.
Nom.	रेणु	रेणु
Acc.	रेणूस-ला-तें	रेणूंस-ला-तें-ना
Inst.	रेणूनें-शीं	रेणूंनीं-हीं-शीं
Dat.	रेणूस-ला-तें	रेणूंस-ला-तें-ना
Abl.	रेणूपासून-हून	रेणूंपासून-हून
Gen.	रेणूचा-ची-चें	रेणूंचा-ची-चें
Loc.	रेणूंत	रेणूंन
Voc.	रेणू	रेणूंनो

घर (*n.*) a house.

Case.	Sing.	Plu.
Nom.	घर	घरें
Acc.	घरांला-स-तें	घरांला-स-तें-ना
Inst.	घरानें-शीं	घरानीं-हीं-शीं
Dat.	घरास-ला-तें	घरांला-स-तें-ना
Abl.	घरापासून-हून	घरांपासून-हून
Gen.	घराचा-ची-चें	घरांचा-ची-चें
Loc.	घरांत	घरांत
Voc.	घरा	घरांनो

Third Declension.

The third declension contains those nouns which in inflection change the last vowel into या yâ. It comprises masculine nouns in आ â, and neuter nouns in ऍ e.

गाडा (m.) a waggon.

Case.	Sing.	Plu.
Nom.	गाडा	गाडे
Acc.	गाड्यास-ला-तें	गाड्यास-ला-तें-ना
Inst.	गाड्यानें-शीं	गाड्यानीं-हीं-शीं
Dat.	गाड्यास-ला-तें	गाड्यास-ला-तें-ना
Abl.	गाड्यापासून-हून	गाड्यापासून-हून
Gen.	गाड्याचा-ची-चें	गाड्याचा-ची-चें
Loc.	गाड्यांत	गाड्यांत
Voc.	गाड्या	गाड्यांनों

तळें (n.) a pond.

Case.	Sing.	Plu.
Nom.	तळें	तळीं
Acc.	तळ्यास-ला-तें	तळ्यास-ला-तें-ना
Inst.	तळ्यानें-शीं	तळ्यानीं-हीं-शीं
Dat.	तळ्यास-ला-तें	तळ्यास-ला-तें-ना
Abl.	तळ्यापासून-हून	तळ्यापासून-हून
Gen.	तळ्याचा-ची-चें	तळ्याचा-ची-चें
Loc.	तळ्यांत	तळ्यांत
Voc.	तळ्या	तळ्यांनों

Fourth Declension.

The fourth declension contains nouns which in inflection change the last vowel of the crude form into ए e. It comprises feminine nouns ending in आ â, and some in अ a.

पागा (*f.*) a stable.

Case.	Sing.	Plu.
Nom.	पागा	पागा
Acc.	पागेस-ला-तें	पागांस-ला-तें-नां
Inst.	पागेनें-शीं	पागांनीं-हीं-शीं
Dat.	पागेस-ला-तें	पागांस-ला-तें-नां
Abl.	पागेपासून-हून	पागांपासून-हून
Gen.	पागेचा-ची-चें	पागांचा-ची-चें
Loc.	पागेंत	पागांत
Voc.	पागे	पागांनों

जीभ (*f.*) tongue.

Case.	Sing.	Plu.
Nom.	जीभ	जिभा
Acc.	जिभेस-ला-तें	जिभांस-ला-तें-नां
Inst.	जिभेनें-शीं	जिभांनीं-हीं-शीं
Dat.	जिभेस-ला-तें	जिभांस-ला-तें-नां
Abl.	जिभेपासून-हून	जिभांपासून-हून
Gen.	जिभेचा-ची-चें	जिभांचा-ची-चें
Loc.	जिभेंत	जिभांत
Voc.	जिभे	जिभांनों

Fifth Declension.

The fifth declension contains nouns which in inflection change the last vowel of the crude form into ई î. It comprises feminine nouns ending in अ a :—

आग (*f.*) fire.

Case.	Sing.	Plu.
Nom.	आग	आगा
Acc.	आगीस-ला-तें	आगींस-ला-तें
Inst.	आगीनें-शीं	आगींनीं-हीं-शीं
Dat.	आगीस-ला-तें	आगींस-ला-तें
Abl.	आगीपासून-हून	आगींपासून-हून
Gen.	आगीचा-ची-चें	आगींचा-ची-चें
Loc.	आगींत	आगींत
Voc.	आग	आगानों

Sixth Declension.

The sixth declension contains those nouns which in inflection change the last vowel of the crude form into आ â. It comprises masculine and neuter nouns in उ û, and some masculine numerals in ए e :—

तट्टू (*n.*) a pony.

Case.	Sing.	Plu.
Nom.	तट्टू	तट्टें
Acc.	तट्टास-ला-तें	तट्टांस-ला-तें-ना
Inst.	तट्टानें-शीं	तट्टांनीं-हीं-शीं
Dat.	तट्टास-ला-तें	तट्टांस-ला-तें-ना

Case.	Sing.	Plu.
Abl.	तट्टापासून-हून	तट्टापास-हून
Gen.	तट्टाचा-ची-चें	तट्टाचा-ची-चें
Loc.	तट्टांत	तट्टांत
Voc.	तट्टा	तट्टांनों

N.B.—No distinction is to be made between उ and ऊ in this declension.

Seventh Declension.

The seventh declension contains those nouns which in inflection change the last vowel of the crude form into its corresponding semivowel. It comprises nouns ending in ई î, ईं în; उ û, ऊं ûn.

मोतीं (*n.*) a pearl.

Case.	Sing.	Plu.
Nom.	मोतीं	मोत्यें or मोतें
Acc.	मोत्यास-ला-नें	मोत्यास-ला-नें-नां
Inst.	मोत्यानें-शीं	मोत्यानीं-हीं-इीं
Dat.	मोत्यास-ला-नें	मोत्यास-ला-नें-नां
Abl.	मोत्यापासून-हून	मोत्यापासून-हून
Gen.	मोत्याचा-चीं-चें	मोत्याचा-ची-चें
Loc.	मोत्यांत	मोत्यांत
Voc.	मोत्या	मोत्यांनों

तारूं (n.) a ship.

Case.	Sing.	Plu.
Nom.	तारूं	तारवें
Acc.	तारवांस-ला-ते	तारवांना-ला-ते-स
Inst.	तारवांने-शीं	तारवांनीं-हीं-शीं
Dat.	तारवांस-ला-ते	तारवांस-ला-ते
Abl.	तारवांपासून-हून	तारवांपासून-हून
Gen.	तारवांचा-ची-चें	तारवांचा-ची-चें
Loc.	तारवांत	तारवांत
Voc.	तारवां	तारवांनों

N.B.—The inflected forms of तारूं may be spelt as above with réph, or with the र; ex. तारवांस or तारवास.

PRONOUNS.

In Maráthi there are five classes of pronouns :— Personal, Demonstrative, Relative, Interrogative, and Indefinite.

PERSONAL PRONOUNS.

मी I.

Case.	Sing.	Plu.
Nom.	मी	आम्ही
Acc.	मला	आम्हांस-ला-ते
Inst.	मीं	आम्हीं आम्हांशीं
Dat.	मला	आम्हांस-ला-ते
Abl.	जमहून-पासून	आम्हाहून, आमच्याहून
Gen.	माझा-झी-झें	आमचा-ची-चें
Loc.	माइयांत	आम्हांत, आमच्यांत

N.B.—The following cases are sometimes written—

Case..	Sing.
Accusative	मजला, मांतें, मज.
Instrumental	म्यां, मजशीं, मशीं.
Dative	As in the Accusative.
Ablative	माझ्याहून.

तूं Thou.

Case.	Sing.	Plu.
Nom.	तूं	तुम्ही
Acc.	तुला	तुम्हांस-ला-तें
Inst.	तूं	तुम्हीं, तुम्हांशीं
Dat.	तुला	तुम्हांस-ला-तें
Abl.	तुजहून-पासून	तुम्हांहून, तुमच्याहून
Gen.	तुझा-झो-झें	तुमचा-ची-चें
Loc.	तुइयांत	तुम्हांत, तुमच्यांत

N.B.—The following cases are sometimes written—

Case.	Sing.
Accusative	तुजला, तुर्तें, तुज.
Instrumental	त्वां-तुजशीं.
Dative	As in the Accusative.
Ablative	तुइयाहून.

तो He, तें It.

Case.	Sing.		Plu.	
	m.	n.	m.	n.
Nom.	तो	तें	ते	तीं
Acc.	त्यास-ला-तें		त्यांना-ला-तें	
Inst.	त्यानें-शीं		त्यांनीं-हीं-शीं	
Dat.	त्याला-स-तें		त्यांना-ला-तें	

Case.	Sing.	Plu.
Abl.	त्यापासुन-हून	त्यांपासून-हून
Gen.	त्याचा-ची-चें	त्यांचा-ची-चें
Loc.	त्यांत	त्यांत

N.B.—The following cases are sometimes written—

Case.	Sing.	Plu.
Acc.	त्याजला	त्यांजला
Inst.	त्यानें, त्याजञीं	त्यांनीं, त्यांजशीं
Dat.	त्याजला	त्यांजला
Abl.	त्याजहून-पासून	त्यांजहून-पासून
Loc.	त्याच्यांत	त्यांच्यांत

ती She.

Case.	Sing.	Plu.
Nom.	ती	त्या
Acc.	तिला-तीस-तिर्ते	त्यांस-नां-तें
Inst.	तिनें-शीं	त्यांनीं-हीं-शीं
Dat.	तिला-तीस-तिर्ते	त्यांस-नां-तें-ला
Abl.	तिइन	त्यांइन
Gen.	तिचा-ची-चें	त्यांचा-ची-चें
Loc.	तींत	त्यांत

N.B.—The following cases are sometimes written—

Case.	Sing.	Plu.
Acc.	तिजला	त्यांजला
Inst.	तिनें, तिजशीं, तिच्याशीं	त्यांनीं, त्यांजशीं, त्यांच्याशीं
Dat.	As in the Acc.	As in the Acc.
Abl.	तिजहून, तिच्याहून	त्यांजहून, त्यांच्याहून
Loc.	तिच्यांत	त्यांच्यांत

m. f. n.

असला-ली-लें such.

Case.	Sing.		Plu.	
	m.	*n.*	*m.*	*n.*
Nom.	असला	असलें	असले	असलीं
Acc.	असल्यास-ला-ने		असल्यांस-ते-नां-ला	
Inst.	असल्याने-शीं		असल्यानीं-शीं-हीं	
Dat.	असल्यास-ला-ने		असल्यांस-ते-नां-ला	
Abl.	असल्यापासून-हून		असल्यांपासून-हून	
Gen.	असल्याचा-ची-चें		असल्यांचा-ची-चें	
Loc.	असल्यांत		असल्यांत	

असली is declined like अशी

असलाला such, इतका so great as, तितका so great as, जितका as great as, एवढा so great, तेवढा so great, केवढा how great, are all declined like असला (*m.*), ली (*f.*), लें (*n.*).

RELATIVE PRONOUNS.

जो-जी-जें who or what.

Case.	Sing.			Plu.		
	m. n.		*f.*	*m. f. n.*		
Nom.	जो	जें	जी	जे	ज्या	जीं
Acc.	ज्यास-ला-ने		जिला-ने, जीस	ज्यांस-ला-ने		
Inst.	ज्याने-शीं-हीं		जिणे-शीं	ज्यानीं-शीं-हीं		
Dat.	ज्यास-ला-ने		जिला-ने, जीस	ज्यांस-ला-ने		
Abl.	ज्याहून-पासून		जिजहून-पासून	ज्यांहून-पासून		
Gen.	ज्याचा-ची-चें		जिचा-ची-चें	ज्यांचा-ची-चें		
Loc.	ज्यांत		जींत	ज्यांत, ज्यांच्यांत		

N.B.—The following cases are sometimes written—

Case.	Sing.	Plu.
Acc.	जाला-स	जानां-स
Inst.	जानें-नें	जांहीं-नीं
Abl.	जाहून	जाहून
Gen.	जांचा	जांचा
Loc.	जांत	जांत

INTERROGATIVE PRONOUNS.

कोण (*m. f.*) who ; काय (*n.*) what.

Case.	Sing. (*m. f.*)	Plu.
Nom.	कोण	कोण
Acc.	कोणाला-स	कोणांस-लां-नें
Inst.	कोणीं-णें-कोणाशीं	कोणांशीं, कोणीं
Dat.	कोणाला-स	कोणाला-स
Abl.	कोणापासून-हून	कोणांपासून-हून
Gen.	कोणाचा-ची-चें	कोणांचा-ची-चें
Loc.	कोणांत	कोणांत

                                              Sing.   Plu.

N.B.—The Loc. is sometimes written कोणाच्यांत कोणांच्यांत

काय (*n.*) what.

Case.	Sing.	Plu.
Nom.	काय	काय
Acc.	कशास-ला-नें	कशांस-लां-नें
Inst.	कशानें-शीं	कशानीं-शीं
Dat.	कशास-ला-नें	कशांस-लां-ना
Abl.	कशाहून-पासून	कशाहून-पासून
Gen.	कशाचा-ची-चें	कशांचा-ची-चें
Loc.	कशांत	कशांत

कसा, कशी, कसें, of what kind, declined like the demonstrative pronoun असा, अशी, असें.

कोणता-ती-तें which, is declined like the demonstrative pronoun असला-ली-लें.

INDEFINITE PRONOUNS.

आपण one's self.

Case.	Plu.
Nominative	आपण
Accusative	आपणांस-ला-तें
Instrumental	आपण, आपणांशीं
Dative	आपणांस-ला-तें
Ablative	आपणांहून-पासून
Genitive	आपला-ली-लें
Locative	आपणांत

N.B.—The following cases are sometimes written—

Acc.	आपल्यास-ला-तें	or	आपल्यास-ला-तें
Inst.	आपल्यांनीं-शीं	,,	आपल्यानें
Dat.	आपल्यास-ला-तें	,,	आपल्यास-ला-तें
Abl.	आपल्यांपासून-हून	,,	आपल्यापासून-हून
Loc.	आपल्यांत		

किती some, *or*, how many, is indeclinable.

कित्येक some one.

Case.	Sing.	Plu.
Nom.	कित्येक	कित्येक
Acc.	कित्येकास-ला-तें	कित्येकांस-नां-ला-तें
Inst.	कित्येकानें-शीं	कित्येकांनीं-हीं-शीं
Dat.	कित्येकास-ला-तें	कित्येकांस-ला-नां
Abl.	कित्येकाहून-पासून	कित्येकांहून-पासून
Gen.	कित्येकाचा-ची-चें	कित्येकांचा-ची-चें
Loc.	कित्येकांत	कित्येकांत

N.B.—The Nom. is sometimes written कितीक or कितीएक

अमका some one, अमकें some thing.

Case.	Sing.		Plu.	
	m.	*n.*	*m.*	*n.*
Nom.	अमका	अमकें	अमके	अमकीं
Acc.	अमक्यास-ला-तें		अमक्यांनां-ला-तें	
Inst.	अमक्यानें-शीं		अमक्यांनीं-हीं-शीं	
Dat.	अमक्यास-ला-तें		अमक्यांस-ला-नां	
Abl.	अमक्यापासून-हून		अमक्यांपासून-हून	
Gen.	अमक्याचा-ची-चें		अमक्यांचा-ची-चें	
Loc.	अमक्यांत		अमक्यांत	

अमकी (*f.*) some one.

Case.	Sing.	Plu.
Nom.	अमकी	अमक्या
Acc.	अमकीस-ला-तें	अमक्यांस-ला-तें-नां
Inst.	अमकीनें-शीं	अमक्यांनीं-हीं

कसा, कशी, कसें, of what kind, declined like the demonstrative pronoun असा, अशी, असें.

कोणता-ती-तें which, is declined like the demonstrative pronoun असला-ली-लें.

INDEFINITE PRONOUNS.

आपण one's self.

Case.	Plu.
Nominative	आपण
Accusative	आपणांस-ला-नें
Instrumental	आपण, आपणांशीं
Dative	आपणांस-ला-नें
Ablative	आपणांहून-पासून
Genitive	आपला-ली-लें
Locative	आपणांन

N.B.—The following cases are sometimes written—

Acc.	आपल्यांस-ला-नें	or	आपल्यास-ला-नें
Inst.	आपल्यांनीं-शीं	,,	आपल्यानें
Dat.	आपल्यांस-ला-नें	,,	आपल्यास-ला-नें
Abl.	आपल्यांपासून-हून	,,	आपल्यापासून-हून
Loc.	आपल्यांत		

किती some, *or*, how many, is indeclinable.

कित्येक some one.

Case.	Sing.	Plu.
Nom.	कित्येक	कित्येक
Acc.	कित्येकांस-ला-तें	कित्येकांस-नां-ला-तें
Inst.	कित्येकानें-शीं	कित्येकांनीं-हीं-शीं
Dat.	कित्येकांस-ला-तें	कित्येकांस-ला-नां
Abl.	कित्येकाहून-पासून	कित्येकांहून-पासून
Gen.	कित्येकाचा-ची-चें	कित्येकांचा-ची-चें
Loc.	कित्येकांत	कित्येकांत

N.B.—The Nom. is sometimes written कितीक or कितीएक

अमका some one, अमकें some thing.

Case.	Sing.		Plu.	
	m.	*n.*	*m.*	*n.*
Nom.	अमका	अमकें	अमके	अमकीं
Acc.	अमक्यास-ला-तें		अमक्यांना-ला-तें	
Inst.	अमक्यानें-शीं		अमक्यांनीं-हीं-शीं	
Dat.	अमक्यास-ला-तें		अमक्यांस-ला-नां	
Abl.	अमक्यापासून-हून		अमक्यांपासून-हून	
Gen.	अमक्याचा-ची-चें		अमक्यांचा-ची-चें	
Loc.	अमक्यांत		अमक्यांत	

अमकी (*f.*) some one.

Case.	Sing.	Plu.
Nom.	अमकी	अमक्या
Acc.	अमकीस-ला-तें	अमक्यांस-ला-तें-नां
Inst.	अमकीनें-शीं	अमक्यांनीं-हीं

Case.	Sing.	Plu.
Dat.	अमकीस-ला-तें	अमक्यांस-ला-नं
Abl.	अमकोपासून-हून	अमक्यांपासून-हून
Gen.	अमकीचा-ची-चें	अमक्यांचा-ची-चें
Loc.	अमकींत	अमक्यांत

तमका-की-कें, some one, is declined like अमका-की-कें.

ADJECTIVES.

An adjective is that which limits the signification of the substantive to which it is attached.

Adjectives denote either quality or quantity.

Adjectives of quantity are called numerals.

Adjectives have number, gender, and case.

When an adjective which in the nominative case ends in आ (*m.*), ई (*f.*), एं (*n.*), agrees with a noun in an inflected case, the adjective ends in या in the singular, and in यां in the plural.

N.B.—This rule is almost universal ; but according to Dâdobâ (*vide* Dâdobâ's Grammar, 3rd edition, p. 140) it is not quite so. Almost all the other adjectives remain unchanged, whatever the number, gender, or case of the substantives with which they agree may be ; ex. एक in any other case but the nominative becomes एका.

Adjectives in Marâthi have no degrees of comparison. The noun which is the object of comparison takes in the comparative degree the base form having पेक्षां or हून affixed ; ex. घोड्या पेक्षां हत्ती मोठा आहे the elephant is bigger than the horse; and in the superlative degree the noun in the base form having आत or मध्यें affixed; ex. सर्वांत तो चांगला आहे he is best of all.

Inferiority is expressed by कमी less, the noun being put into the ablative case; ex. मजहून तो कमी बळकट आहे he is less strong than I am. Slight diminution is expressed by adding सर or सा (*m.*), शी (*f.*), सें (*n.*) to the adjective; ex. लहानसा a little small.

N.B.—A few adjectives derived from Sanscrit take the Sanscrit terminations in comparison; ex. लघुतर a little smaller, लघुतम the least.

CARDINAL NUMBERS.

The cardinal numbers in Marâṭhi may be seen in the following table:—

1	१	एक.	16	१६	सोळा.
2	२	दोन.	17	१७	सत्रा.
3	३	तीन.	18	१८	अठरा.
4	४	चार.	19	१९	एकुणीस.
5	५	पांच.	20	२०	वीस.
6	६	सहा.	21	२१	एकवीस.
7	७	सात.	22	२२	बावीस, बेवीस.
8	८	आठ.	23	२३	तेवीस.
9	९	नऊ.	24	२४	चोवीस, चौवीस.
10	१०	दहा.	25	२५	पंचवीस.
11	११	अकरा.	26	२६	सव्वीस.
12	१२	बारा.	27	२७	सत्तावीस.
13	१३	तेरा.	28	२८	अठ्ठावीस.
14	१४	चवदा, चौदा.	29	२९	एकुणतीस.
15	१५	पंधरा.	30	३०	तीस.

31	३१	एकतीस.	60 ६०	साठ.
32	३२	बत्तीस.	61 ६१	एकसष्ट.
33	३३	तेंतीस, तेहतीस.	62 ६२	बासष्ट.
34	३४	चवतीस, चौंतीस.	63 ६३	त्रेसष्ट.
35	३५	पस्तीस.	64 ६४	चवसष्ट, चौसष्ट.
36	३६	छत्तीस.	65 ६५	पांसष्ट.
37	३७	सदतीस, सतनीस.	66 ६६	सासष्ट.
38	३८	अडतीस.	67 ६७	सदसष्ट, सत्सष्ट.
39	३९	एकुणचाळीस.	68 ६८	अडसष्ट, अडुसष्ट.
40	४०	चाळीस, चाळ, ताळ.	69 ६९	एकुणहत्तर.
41	४१	एकेचाळीस.	70 ७०	सत्तर.
42	४२	बेचाळीस.	71 ७१	एक्काहत्तर.
43	४३	त्रेचाळीस.	72 ७२	बाहत्तर.
44	४४	चव्वेचाळीस.	73 ७३	त्रेहत्तर, त्र्याहत्तर.
45	४५	पंचेचाळीस.	74 ७४	चौंऱ्याहत्तर, चौरेहत्तर.
46	४६	शेचाळीस.	75 ७५	पंचेहत्तर.
47	४७	सत्तेचाळीस.	76 ७६	शाहत्तर.
48	४८	अठेचाळीस.	77 ७७	सत्याहत्तर, सत्तेहत्तर.
49	४९	एकुणपन्नास.	78 ७८	अठ्याहत्तर, अठ्ठेहत्तर.
50	५०	पन्नास.	79 ७९	एकुणऐंशीं.
51	५१	एकावन्न.	80 ८०	ऐंशीं.
52	५२	बावन्न.	81 ८१	एक्यांयशीं, एक्केऐंशीं.
53	५३	त्रेपन्न.	82 ८२	ब्यायशीं, ब्याएंशीं.
54	५४	चौपन्न, चोपन्न.	83 ८३	ल्यायशीं, ल्याऐंशीं.
55	५५	पंचावन्न.	84 ८४	चौंऱ्यायशीं, चवऱ्यांऐंशीं.
56	५६	छपन्न.	85 ८५	पचाय्शीं.
57	५७	सत्तावन्न.	86 ८६	शाय्शीं.
58	५८	अठ्ठावन्न.	87 ८७	सत्याय्शीं.
59	५९	एकुणसाठ.	88 ८८	अठ्ठ्यांय्शीं.

89	८९	एकुणनव्वद, नव्यांश्शीं	95	९५	पंचाण्णव.
90	९०	नव्वद.	96	९६	शाण्णव.
91	९१	एक्याण्णव.	97	९७	सत्याण्णव.
92	९२	ब्याण्णव.	98	९८	अठ्याण्णव.
93	९३	त्याण्णव	99	९९	नव्याण्णव.
94	९४	चौऱ्याण्णव.	100	१००	शंभर.
101	१०१	एकोत्तरशें, एकशें एक.			
102	१०२	दुवोत्तरशें, एकशें दोन.			
200	२००	दोनशें.			
300	३००	तीनशें.			
500	५००	पांचशें.			
1,000	१०००	हजार, सहस्र.			
10,000	१००००	दहाहजार, दशसहस्र.			
100,000	१०००००	लाख, लक्ष.			
1,000,000	१००००००	दहालाख, दशलक्ष.			
10,000,000	१०००००००	कोट, क्रोड.			

दोन, तीन, चार, are declined as follows:—

	दोन Two.	तीन Three.
Case.	Plu.	Plu.
Nom.	दोन	तीन
Acc.	दोहोंस-ला-तें-ना	तीहींस-ला-तें-ना
Inst.	दोहोंनीं-हीं-शीं	तीहोंनीं-हीं-शीं
Dat.	दोहोंस-ला-तें-ना	तीहींस-ला-तें-ना
Abl.	दोहोंपासून-हून	तीहींपासून-हून
Gen.	दोहोंचा-ची-चें	तीहीं चा-ची-चें
Loc.	दोहोंत	तीहींत

3 M G*

चार. Four.

Case.	Plu.	Case.	Plu.
Nom.	चार	Abl.	चोहोंपासून-हून
Acc.	चोहोंस-ला-ते-ना	Gen.	चोहोंचा-चो-चें
Inst.	चोहोंनीं-हीं-शीं	Loc.	चोहोंत
Dat.	चोहोंस-ला-ते-ना		

दोघे, दोघी, दोघें, both; उभयतां both; तिघे, तिघी, तिघें, all three; चौघे, चौघी, चौघें, all four.

	दोघे	दोघी
Case.	Plu.	Plu.
	m. n.	f.
Nom.	दोघे, दोघें	दोघी
Acc.	दोघांस-ला-ना	दोघींस-ला-ना
Inst.	दोघानीं-हीं-शीं	दोघींनीं-हीं-शीं
Dat.	दोघांस-ला-ते-ना	दोघींस-ला-ते-ना
Abl.	दोघांपासून-हून	दोघींपासून-हून
Gen.	दोघांचा-चो-चें	दोघींचा-चो-चें
Loc.	दोघांत	दोघींत

N.B.—दोघे, तिघे, चौघे, are applied generally to human beings. They are also sometimes applied to other animate objects.

ORDINAL NUMBERS.

m. f. n.		m. f. n.	
पहिला -ली -लें,	first.	साहवा -वी -वें,	sixth.
दुसरा -री -रें,	second.	सातवा -वी -वें,	seventh.
निसरा -री -रें,	third.	आठवा -वी -वें,	eighth.
चौथा -थी -थें,	fourth.	नववा -वी -वें,	ninth.
पांचवा -वी -वें,	fifth.	दाहवा -वी -वें,	tenth.

These are all declined like the demonstrative pronoun असला-ली-लें.

FRACTIONAL NUMBERS.

$\frac{1}{4}$	·l·	पाव.
$\frac{1}{2}$	·ll·	अर्धां-र्धी-र्धें &c.
$\frac{3}{4}$	·lll·	पाऊण.
$1\frac{1}{4}$	१l·	सव्वा.
$1\frac{1}{2}$	१ll·	दीड.
$1\frac{3}{4}$	१lll·	पावणेदोन, पाउणेदोन.
$2\frac{1}{4}$	२l·	सव्वादोन.
$2\frac{1}{2}$	२ll·	अडीच.
$2\frac{3}{4}$	२lll·	पावणेतीन, पाउणेतीन.
$3\frac{1}{4}$	३l·	सव्वातीन.
$3\frac{1}{2}$	३ll·	साडेतीन.
$3\frac{3}{4}$	३lll·	पावणेचार पाउणेचार.

VERBS.

Verb is the grammatical term for *action*. Verbs are either transitive or intransitive.

The only complete voice in Marâthi is the active. The passive is formed for the most part by the addition of the verb जाणें; ex. तो मारला जातो He is beaten. Some few verbs though active in form have a middle signification; ex. तो वाकतो He bends himself.

MOODS.

In Marâthi there are four moods:—Indicative, Imperative, Subjunctive, and Potential.

Those forms which assert directly are said to be in the indicative mood; ex. तें तो करितो He does that.

The imperative mood commands, requests, or prays; ex. तें कर Do that; ईश्वर तुझें कल्याण करो May God bless you!

Assertions that are in sense conditional are put in the subjunctive mood; ex. तूं असें केलें तर मी तुला शिक्षा करीन If you were to do that I should punish you.

The potential mood is that which expresses capability, power, or duty; ex. तें माझ्यानें करवतें I can do that; आपण आतां जावें you ought to go now.

Tense.

The tenses of a verb show the time of the thing asserted.

अस (which is the root of असणें) to be.

INDICATIVE MOOD.

Present Tense, I am.

Sing.		*Plu.*	
मी	आहें	आम्ही	आहों
तूं	आहेस	तुम्ही आहां, आहांत	
तो ⎫		ते ⎫	
ती ⎬	आहे	त्या ⎬	आहेत
तें ⎭		तीं ⎭	

N.B.—Besides the above, there are two other forms of this tense in use: I. होय (generally used in definitions—sometimes used to give emphasis); II. असतों (used to express habit).

Sing.		Plu.	
मी	होय	आम्ही	हों
तूं	होस	तुम्ही	व्हा
तो	⎫	ते	⎫
ती	⎬ होय	त्या	⎬ होत
तें	⎭	तीं	⎭

	Sing.			Plu.	
	m.	f.	n.	m. f. n.	
1.	असतों	-यें	-तें	असतों	
2.	असतोस	-येस	-तेंस	असतां	
3.	असतो	-ये	-तें	असतात	

N.B.—In the Desh the following forms are also to be found in use :—

असतीस for असत्येंस
असती ,, असत्ये

Some writers use the following forms :—

असतें for असत्यें
असतेस ,, असत्येंस
असते ,, असत्ये

Present Prospective, I am being.

	Sing.	Plu.
1.	असत आहें	असत आहों
2.	असत आहेस	असत आहां
3.	असत आहे	असत आहेत

Present Habitual, I am being.

	Sing.			Plu.
	m.	f.	n.	m. f. n.
1.	असन	असतों -त्यें -नें		असत असतों
2.	असन	असतोस -त्येस -नेस		असत असतां
3.	असत	असनों -त्यें -नें		असत असतान

Present Perfect.

This tense is not found in the verb असणें. Its place is supplied by वसलों आहें, I have been and am sitting.

Present Prospective, I am about to be.

	Sing.	Plu.
1.	असणार आहें	असणार आहों
2.	असणार आहेस	असणार आहां
3.	असणार आहे	असणार आहेत

Past, I was.

	Sing.			Plu.		
	m.	f.	n.	m.	f.	n.
1.	होतों	-त्यें	-तं	होतां	-तीं	-नीं
2.	होतास	-तीस	-तेस	होतां	-तां	-तां
3.	होता	-ती	-तें	होने	-त्या	-तीं

N.B.—The second person plural is sometimes written:

m.	f.	n.
होनेन	हांतींत, -त्यात	होनींत

Past Progressive, I was being.

	Sing.			*Plural.*		
	m.	f.	n.	m.	f.	n.
1.	असत होतों	-यें	-तें	असत होतों	-तों	-तों
2.	असत होतास	-तीस	-तेंस	असत होतां	-ताં	-ताં
3.	असत होता	-ती	-तें	असत होते	-त्या	-तीं

Past Habitual, I was being.

	Sing.	*Plu.*
1.	असें	असूं
2.	असस	असां
3.	असे	असत.

Pluperfect, I had been.

Sing.

	m.	f.	n.
1.	असलों होतों	असल्यें होत्यें	असलें होतें
2.	असला -तास	असली -तीस	असलें -नेंस
3.	असला -ता	असली -ती	असलें -नें

Plu.

1. असलों-व्या-लीं होतों
2. असला-ला-ला होतां
3. असले होते -ह्या होत्या -लीं होतीं

Complete Perfect, I began and was.

N.B.—This tense has an inceptive, continuative, and completive force.

Sing.

	m.	f.	n.
1.	असता झालों	असत्यें झाल्यें	असतें झालें
2.	असता झालास	असती झालीस	असतें झालेंस
3.	असता झाला	असतो झाली	असतें झालें

Plu.

1.	असते झालों	असत्या झालों	असतीं झालों
2.	असना झालां	असऱ्या झालां	असतीं झालां
3.	असते झाले	असत्या झाल्या	असतीं झालीं

Past Prospective, I was about to be.

Sing. *Plu.*

	m.	f.	n.	
1.	असणार होतों	-यें	-तें	असणार होतों
2.	असणार होतास	-तीस	-नेस	असणार होतां
3.	असणार होता	-ती	-नें	असणार होते-त्या-तीं

Future Tense, I will be.

Sing. *Plu.*

1.	असेन	असूं
2.	असशील	असाल
3.	असेल	असतील

Progressive Future, I shall go on being.

Sing. *Plu.*

1.	असत असेन	असत असूं
2.	असन असशील	असत असाल
3.	असत असेल	असन असनील

Future Perfect, I shall have been.

	Sing.			Plu.	
m.	f.	n.	m.	f.	n.
1. असलों -ल्यें -लें असेन			असलों -ल्या -लीं असूं		
2. असला -ली -लें असशील			असले -ल्या -लीं असाल		
3. असला -ली -लें असेल			असेल -ल्या -लीं असतील		

IMPERATIVE MOOD, Let me be.

Sing.	Plu.
1. असूं	असूं
2. अस or ऐस	असा
3. असो	असोत

SUBJUNCTIVE MOOD.

Past Tense, I should be or have been.

	Sing.			Plu.	
m.	f.	n.	m.	f.	n.
1. असतों -त्यें -तें			असतों -तीं -तीं		
2. असतास -तीस -तेंस			असतां -तां -तां		
3. असता -ती -तें			असते -त्या -तीं		

N.B.—The 2nd person plural is also written:

m.　f. n.

असतेत　असतींत.

Past Progressive, I should be being.

	Sing.			Plu.	
m.	f.	n.	m.	f.	n.
1. असत असतों -त्यें -तें			असत असतों -तीं-तीं		
2. असत असतास -तीस -तेंस			असत असतां -तां -तां		
3. असत असता -ती -तें			असत असते -त्या -तीं		

Pluperfect, I should have been.

Sing.

	m.	f.	n.
1.	असलों असतों,	असल्यें असल्यं,	असलें असतें
2.	असला असतास,	असली असतीस,	असलें असतेंस
3.	असला असना,	असली असती,	असलें असतें

Plu.

1.	असलों असतों,	असल्या असतों,	असलीं असतां
2.	असलां असतां		
3.	असले असते,	असल्या असत्या,	असलीं असतीं

POTENTIAL MOOD.

Present Tense.

I may, can, might, should, or would be.

	Sing.			Plu.		
	m.	f.	n.	m.	f.	n.
1.	भसावा	-वी	-वें	भसावें	-व्या	-वीं
2.	भसावास	-वीस	-वेंस	भसावेत	-व्यान	-वींन
3.	भसावा	-वी	-वें	भसावे	-व्या	-वीं

N.B.—The construction given above is "Active." The "Neuter" construction also may be used; ex. मीं भसावें it is to be by me, *i. e.* I ought to be.

Present Progressive, I ought to be being.

I. मीं भसत भसावें (it ought to be being by me); for the other person *vide* personal pronoun भसत भसावें remaining unchanged throughout.

Present Habitual, I ought to be in the habit of being.

	Sing.			Plu.	
m.	*f.*	*n.*	*m.*	*f.*	*n.*
1. असत असावा	-वी	-वें	असत असावे	-व्या	-वीं
2. असत असावास	-वीस	-वेंस	असत असावेत	-व्यात	-वींत
3. असत असावा	-वी	-वें	असत असावे	-व्या	-वीं

Past, I might be.

Sing.

m.	*f.*	*n.*
1. असायाचा होतों,	-ची होत्यें,	-चें होतें
2. असायाचा होतास,	-ची होतीस,	-चें होतेंस
3. असायाचा होता,	-ची होती,	-चें होतें

Plu.

m.	*f.*	*n.*
1. असायाचे	-च्या	-चीं होतों
2. असायाचे	-च्या	-चीं होतां
3. असायाचे होते,	-च्या होत्या,	-चीं होतीं

N.B.—This tense, like the present, can be used in the "Neuter Construction;" ex. मीं असायाचें होतें it might be by me, *i. e.* I might be.

Future, I may be about to be.

    m. f. n.
1. असणार असावा -वी -वें. For conjugation *vide* the esent Potential.

Infinitive, असूं to be.

Verbal Noun, असणें being *or* to be.

PARTICIPLES.

Present, असत, असतां, असतांनां being.

Compound Present, असलें असतां being in a state of being.

Preterite असून Having been.

      m. *f.* *n.*

Participial Adjective, असलेला -ली -लें being. The participial adjective is declined like the simple adjective.

Future, असणार about to be.

     m. *f.* *n.*

Future Passive, असावा -वी -वें fit to be.

      m. *f.* *n.*

Gerundive, Nom. असावयाचा -ची -चें fit to be.
———— Dat. असावयास to be fit to be.

N.B.—असावयाचा. &c. is sometimes written असायाचा &c., and असावयास as असायास.

VERBAL NOUN.

Case.		
Nom.	असणें	(The act of) being.
Acc.	असण्यास	to be.
Inst.	असण्यानें	by being.
Dat.	असण्यास	to be.
Abl.	असण्यापासून	from being.
Gen.	असण्याचा	of being.
Loc.	असण्यांत	in being.

Negative Form of असणें *to be.*

Present Tense, I am not.

    1st *form.*

   Sing.   *Plu.*
1. नाहीं   नाहीं
2. नाहींस   नाहींत
3. नाहीं   नाहींत

2nd form.

	Sing.	Plu.
1.	नऱ्हें	नऱ्हां
2.	नऱ्हस or नऱ्हेरा	नऱ्हा
3.	नऱ्हे	नव्हत or नऱ्हेत

3rd form.

	Sing. m.	f.	n.	Plu.
1.	नसतों	-त्यें	-तें	नसतों
2.	नसतोस	-त्येस	-तेंस	नसता
3.	नसतो	-त्ये	-तें	नसतात

Past Tense, I was not.

	Sing. m.	f.	n.	Plu. m.	f.	n.
1.	नऱ्हतों	-त्यें	-तें	नऱ्हतों	-तों	-तों
2.	नव्हतास	-तोस	-तेंस	नऱ्हतां	-तां	-तां
3.	नऱ्हता	-ती	-तें	तऱ्हते	-स्या	-तीं

All the other tenses of this verb are regular, and are declined in the same way as those of असणें, the अ being changed into न throughout.

हों (which is the root of होणें) to become.

Present Tense, I become.

	Sing. m.	f.	n.	Plu. m. f. n.
1.	होतों	-त्यें	-तें	होतों
2.	होतोस	-त्येस	-तेंस	होता
3.	होतो	-त्ये	-तें	होतात

Present Progressive, I am becoming.

   Sing.   Plu.

1. होत आहें   होत आहों

For 2nd and 3rd persons *vide* आहें (present tense of अस), होत remaining the same throughout.

Present Habitual, I am in the habit of becoming.

   Sing.   Plu.

   m.   *f.*   *n.*
1. होत असतों -त्यें -तें   होन असतों

For 2nd and 3rd persons *vide* असतों, होत remaining the same throughout.

Present Perfect, I have become.

   Sing.   Plu.

   m.   *n.*
1. ज्ञालों -ह्यें -लें आहें   ज्ञालों आहों
2. ज्ञाला -ली   -लें आहेस   ज्ञाला आहां
3. ज्ञाला -ली   -लें आहे   ज्ञाले -ल्या -लीं आहेत

Present Prospective, I am about to become.

   Sing.   Plu.

1. होणार आहें   होणार आहों

For 2nd and 3rd persons *vide* आहें, होणार remaining unchanged throughout.

Past, I became.

	Sing.			*Plu.*	
m.	*f.*	*n.*	*m.*	*f.*	*n.*
1. झालों	-ल्यें	-लें	झालें	..	..
2. झालास	-लीस	-लेंस	झाला	..	..
3. झाला	-ली	-लें	झाले	-ल्या	-लीं

N.B.—झाला is sometimes written झालात.

Past Progressive, I was becoming.

	Sing.			*Plu.*	
m.	*f.*	*n.*	*m. f. n.*		
1. होत होतों	-त्यें	-तें	होन होतों		

For 2nd and 3rd persons *vide* (past tense) होतों, होन remaining the same throughout.

Past Habitual, I used to become.

	Sing.	*Plu.*
1.	होईं	होऊं
2.	होईस	व्हा
3.	होई	होत

Past Habitual (2nd form).

	Sing.	*Plu.*
1.	होत असें	होत असूं
2.	होत असस	होत असा
3.	होत असे	होत असत

Pluperfect, I had become.

	Sing.			*Plu.*
m.	*f.*	*n.*	*m. f. n.*	
1. झालों होतों, झाल्यें होत्यें, झालें होतें			झालों होतों.	

For 2nd and 3rd persons *vide* झालों and होतों.

Complete Perfect, I began and became.

Sing.

	m.	f.	n.
1.	होतां झालों,	होंय्यें झाल्यें,	होनें झालें
2.	होतां झालास,	होती झालीस,	होनें झालिंस
3.	होतां झाला,	होती झाली,	होनें झालें

Plu.

1.	होंनें झालों	......	......
2.	होनां झालां	......	......
3.	होते झाले,	होंत्या झाल्या,	होनीं झालीं

Past Prospective, I was about to become.

Sing.   *Plu.*

	m.	f.	n.	
1.	होणार होंनों	-त्यें	-नें	होणार होंनों

For 2nd and 3rd persons *vide* होंनों (past tense), होणार remaining unchanged throughout.

Future, I shall become.

	Sing.	*Plu.*
1.	होईन	होऊं
2.	होशील	व्हाल
3.	होईल	होतील

Future Progressive, I shall be becoming.

	Sing.	*Plu.*
1.	होंत असेन	होंत असूं

For 2nd and 3rd persons *vide* असेन, होंत remaining unchanged throughout.

Future Perfect, I shall have become.

   Sing.   Plu.

  m. f. n.

1. झालों -ल्यें -लें असेन झालों अमूं

For 2nd and 3rd persons *vide* झालों and असेन.

Future Prospective, I shall be about to become.

   Sing.   Plu.

1. होणार असेन   होणार अमूं

For 2nd and 3rd persons *vide* असेन, होणार remaining unchanged throughout.

IMPERATIVE MOOD, Let me become.

   Sing.   Plu.

 1. होऊं   होऊं
 2. हो   व्हा
 3. होऊ   होऊत

N.B.—The 3rd person singular and plural are sometimes written होवो and होवोत.

SUBJUNCTIVE MOOD.

Past Tense, I should become or have become.

    Sing.   Plu.

  m. f. n. m. f. n.

1. होतों -त्यें -तें होतों .. ..
2. होतास -तीस -तेंस होतां .. ..
3. होता -ती -तें होते -त्या -तीं

Past Progressive, I should have been becoming.

	Sing.			Plu.
	m.	f.	n.	m. f. n.
1.	होत असतों	-त्यें	-तें	होत असतों.

For 2nd and 3rd persons *vide* असतों (present subjunctive), होत remaining unchanged throughout.

Pluperfect, I should have become.

	Sing.			Plu.
	m.	f.	n.	m. f. n.
1.	झालों असतों,	झाल्यें असत्यें,	झालें असतें.	झालों असतों

For 2nd and 3rd persons *vide* झालों and असतों (subj.).

POTENTIAL MOOD.

Present Tense (Active Construction), I may become.

	Sing.			Plu.		
	m.	f.	n.	m.	f.	n.
1.	व्हादा	-वी	-वें	व्हावे	-व्या	-वीं
2.	व्हावास	-वीस	-वेंस	व्हावे	-व्या	-वीं
3.	व्हावा	-वी	-वें	व्हावे	-व्या	-वीं

Present Tense (Neuter Construction), may become by me.

1. मीं व्हावें. For the other persons *vide* personal pronoun, व्हावें remaining the same throughout.

Present Progressive (also *Habitual*).

I may, can, should be, or should be in the habit of becoming (lit., It may be become by me).

Sing.	Plu.
मीं होत असावें	आम्हीं होत असावें

For 2nd and 3rd persons *vide* the instrumental case of the personal pronouns, होत and असावें remaining unchanged throughout.

N.B.—तूं होत असावेंस is a common way of writing the 2nd person, the final स being probably no more than an intensifying particle.

Present Perfect, I may have become.

Sing.	Plu.
1. झालों असावा	झालों असावे

For 2nd and 3rd persons *vide* झालों and असावा.

Past (Active Construction), I might become.

Sing.

m.	f.	n.
1. व्हावयाचा होतों,	व्हावयाची होतियें,	व्हावयाचें होतें.
&c.	&c.	&c.

Past (Neuter Construction), It might become by me.

Sing.	Plu.
1. मीं व्हायाचें होतें	आम्हीं व्हायाचें होतें

For 2nd and 3rd persons *vide* personal pronoun, व्हायाचें and होतें remaining the same throughout.

Future, I should be about to become.

Sing.			Plu.		
m.	f.	n.	m.	f.	n.
होणार असावा	-वी	-वें	होणार असावे	-व्या	-वीं

For 2nd and 3rd persons *vide* असावा, होणार remaining the same throughout.

Infinitive, होऊं to become.

VERBAL NOUN, होणें the act of becoming.

PARTICIPLES.

Present, होत. होतां. होतांनां becoming.

Compound Present, होत असतां. होत असतांनां being in the state of becoming.

Preterite, होऊन having become.

Compound Past, झालें असतां. झालें असतांनां being in the state of having become.

	m.	f.	n.

Participial Adjective, झालेला -ली -लें.

The participial adjective is declined like the common adjective.

Future, होणार about to become.

	m.	f.	n.

Future Passive, व्हावा -वी -वें fit to become.

	m.	f.	n.

Gerundive, Nom. व्हायाचा -ची -चें fit to become.

„ Dat. व्हायास to become fit to become.

N.B.— व्हायाचा &c. is sometimes written व्हावयाचा &c., and व्हायास as व्हावयास.

VERBAL NOUN.

Case.	Sing.	Plu.
Nom.	होणें becoming.	होणीं
Acc.	होण्यास to become.	होण्यांस

Case.	Sing.		Plu.
Inst.	होण्याने	by becoming.	होण्यानीं
Dat.	होण्यास	to become.	होण्यास
Abl.	होण्यापासून	from becoming.	होण्यापासून
Gen.	होण्याचा	of becoming.	होण्याचा
Loc.	होण्यांत	in becoming.	होण्यांत

Negative Form of होणें *to become.*

Indicative Mood.

Tense.		
Present.	मी होत नाहीं	I am not becoming.
Present Habitual.	मी होत नसतों	I am not in the habit of becoming.
Past.	मी झालों नाहीं	I did not become.
Past Progressive.	मी होत नव्हतों	I was not becoming.
Past Habitual.	{मी होईना / मी होत नसें}	I was not in the habit of becoming.
Pluperfect.	मी झालों नव्हतों	I had not become.
Past Prospective.	मी होणार नव्हतों	I was not about to become.
Future.	मी होणार नाहीं	I shall not become.
Future Progressive.	मी होत नसेन	I shall not be becoming.
Future Perfect.	मी झालों नसेन	I shall not have become.
Future Prospective.	मी होणार नसेन	I shall not be about to become.

5 M G

Imperative Mood, Let me not become.

	Sing.	*Plu.*
1.	होऊं नको	होऊं नको
2.	होऊं नको	होऊं नका
3.	{न होऊ न होवो}	{न होऊन न होवोत}

Subjunctive Mood.

Tense.		
Past.	{मी न होतों. मी होतोंना.}	I should not become.
Past Progressive.	मी होत नसतों	I should not be becoming.
Pluperfect.	मी झालों नसतों	I should not have become.

Potential Mood.

Tense.		
Present.	मी होऊं नये	I may not become.
Present Progressive.	{मी होत नसावा मी होत असूं नये}	I may not be becoming.
Present Perfect.	मी झालों नसावा	I may not have become.
Past.	मीं व्हावयाचें नव्हतें	It might not have become by me.
Future.	मी होणार नसावा	I should not be about to become.

The participles, gerunds, &c., are the same as those of the positive verbs with the addition of न; ex. होण्यास to become, न होण्यास not to become.

AUXILIARY VERBS.

In addition to the two auxiliary verbs असणें to be, and होणें to become, the following are in use in Marâthi :—

जाणें to go; ex. असें करित जा go on doing so.
येणें to come; ex. मला चालतां येतें I can walk.
देणें to give; ex. मी तिला बसूं देतों I allow her to sit.
लागणें to begin, or to set to ; तो रडूं लागला he began to cry.
बसणें to sit; तो सदा हसत बसतो he is always laughing.
पाहणें to see; तो त्याचें पागोटें घेऊं पाहतो he tries to get his turban.

These verbs are defective :—
- पाहिजे it is wanted; मला आंबा दिला पाहिजे I must have a mango given to me.
- नको do not; जाऊं नको Do not go.
- नये should not be; शूद्रानें दान घेऊं नये a Shudra should not receive charity.
- नलगे is not necessary; मला ती तरवार घेणें नलगे it is not necessary for me to take that sword.

N.B.—देणें, लागणें, पाहणें, नको, नये require the verbs to which they are auxiliary to be placed in the infinitive of purpose (ऊं).

बसणें and जाणें require the present participle (त).
येणें requires the present participles (त or तां).
पाहिजे requires the past participle passive (ला).
नलगे requires the gerund (ण).

TRANSITIVE VERB कर (which is the root of करणें) to do.

Present Tense, I do *or* make.

	Sing.			Plu.
	m.	f.	n.	
1.	करितों	-त्यें	-तं	करितों
2.	करितोस	-त्येस	-तेंस	करितां
3.	करितो	-त्ये	-तें	करितात

Present Progressive, I am doing.

   Sing.   *Plu.*

 1. करित आहें करित आहां

For 2nd and 3rd persons *vide* आहें, करित remaining the same throughout.

Present Habitual, I am in the habit of doing.

   Sing.   *Plu.*

  m. *f.* *n.* *m. f. n.*

 1. करित असतों -यें -तं करित असतों

For 2nd and 3rd persons *vide* असतों, करित remaining unchanged throughout.

Present Perfect, It has been done by me.

   Sing.   *Plu.*

 m. *f.* *n.* *m.* *f.* *n.*
मीं केला -ली -लें आहे मीं केले -ल्या -लीं आहेत

For 2nd and 3rd persons, &c. *vide* the personal pronoun, which is always to be placed in the instrumental case, whilst the verb agrees in gender and number with its noun.

Present Prospective, I am about to do.

   Sing.   *Plu.*

 1. करणार आहें करणार आहां

For 2nd and 3rd persons *vide* आहें, करणार remaining unchanged throughout.

Past, made by me.

Sing.			Plu.		
m.	f.	n.	m.	f.	n.
1. मीं केला	-ली	-लें	मीं केले	-ल्या	-लीं

For 2nd and 3rd persons *vide* personal pronoun.

Past Progressive, I was doing.

Sing.			Plu.
m.	f.	n.	m. f. n.
1. करित होतों	-त्यें	-तें	करित होतों

For 2nd and 3rd persons *vide* होतों (past tense), करित remaining unchanged throughout.

Past Habitual (1st form), I was in the habit of doing.

1. करीं   करूं
2. करीस   करां
3. करी   करीत

Past Habitual (2nd form).

1. करित असें   करित असूं

For 2nd and 3rd persons *vide* असें, करित remaining the same throughout.

Pluperfect, Had been done by me.

Sing.

m.   f.   n.

मीं केला होता, -ली -ती, -लें -तें

For 2nd and 3rd persons &c. *vide* rule given under the present perfect tense.

Complete Perfect, I began and made.

Sing.

        m.   f.   n.

1. करता झालों, -र्यें -ल्यें, -नें -लें
2. करिता झालास, -ती -लीस, -नें -लेंस
3. करिता झाला, -ती -ली, -नें -लें

Plu.

1. करिते झालों, -र्या -लों, -तीं -लों
2. करिते झालां, -र्या -लां, -तीं -लां
3. करिते झाले, -र्या -ल्या, -तीं -लीं

Past Prospective, I was about to do.

   Sing.   *Plu.*

 m. f. n.   m. f. n.

1. करणार होतों -र्यें -नें   करणार होतों.

For 2nd and 3rd persons *vide* होतों, करणार remaining the same throughout.

Future, I will make.

   Sing.   *Plu.*

1. करीन   करूं
2. करशील   कराल
3. करील   करतील

Future Progressive, I shall be making.

   Sing.   *Plu.*

1. करित असेन   करित असूं
2. करित असशील   करित असाल
3. करित असेल   करित असनील

Future Perfect, shall have been done by me.

Sing.

म. f. n.
मों केला -ली -लें असेल

For 2nd and 3rd persons, &c. *vide* personal pronoun, and असेल.

Future Prospective, I shall be about to do.

1. करणार असेन   करणार असूं

For 2nd and 3rd persons *vide* असेन, करणार remaining the same throughout.

Imperative Mood.

Present Tense, Let me do.

	Sing.	*Plu.*
1.	करूं	करूं
2.	कर	करा
3.	करो	करोत

Subjunctive Mood.

Past Tense, I should do *or* should have done.

	Sing.			*Plu.*		
	m.	f.	n.	m.	f.	n.
1.	करितों	-त्यें	-तें	करितों	..	..
2.	करितास	-तीस	-तेंस	करितां	..	..
3.	करिता	-ती	-तें	करिते	-त्या	-तीं

Past Progressive, I should have been doing *or* should have been in the habit of doing.

	Sing.			*Plu.*
	m.	f.	n.	
1.	करित असतों	-त्यें	-तें	करित असतों

For 2nd and 3rd persons *vide* भसतों (subj.); करित remaining unchanged throughout.

Pluperfect, (Passive Construction), would have been done by me.

    m.   *f.*   *n.*

1. मीं केला भसता, केली भसती, केलें भसतें

For 2nd and 3rd persons *vide* personal pronoun केला and असता (subj.).

Pluperfect (Neuter Construction), It would have been done by me to.

Sing.

1. मीं केलें असतें

For 2nd and 3rd persons *vide* personal pronoun, केलें, and असतें remaining unchanged throughout.

Potential Mood.

Present (Passive Construction), may be done by me.

Sing.

   m.   *f.*   *n.*

1. मीं करावा -वी -वें

For 2nd and 3rd persons, &c. *vide* personal pronoun and करावा.

Present (Neuter Construction), It may be done by me to.

Sing.

1. मीं करावें

For 2nd and 3rd persons *vide* personal pronoun, करावें remaining unchanged throughout.

Present Progressive (Passive Construction) I may, can, should be, *or* should be in the habit of doing.

   Sing.   Plu.

  m. f. n.   m. f. n.

मीं करित भसावा -वी -वें   मीं करित असावें -व्या -वीं

For 2nd and 3rd persons *vide* personal pronoun and भसावा, करित remaining unchanged throughout.

Present Progressive (Neuter Construction), It may, should, &c. be done by me to.

   Sing.

 1.   मीं करित भसावें

For 2nd and 3rd persons, &c. *vide* personal pronoun, करित भसावें remaining unchanged throughout.

Present Perfect (Passive Construction), It may have been done by.

   Sing.

  m.   f.   n.

1.   मीं केला भसावा, केली भसावी, केलें भसावें.

For 2nd and 3rd persons, &c. *vide* personal pronoun केला and भसावा.

Present Perfect (Neuter Construction), It may have been done by me to.

   Sing.

 1.   मीं केलें भसावें

For 2nd and 3rd persons *vide* personal pronoun, केलें भसावें remaining the same throughout.

Past (Passive Construction), ought to *or* might have been done by.

Sing.

m.   *f.*   *n.*

1. मीं करायाचा होता, करायाची होती, करायाचें होतें.

For 2nd and 3rd persons &c. *vide* personal pronoun करायाचा and होता.

Past (Neuter Construction), It ought to *or* might have been done by me to.

Sing.

1. मीं करायाचें होतें.

For 2nd and 3rd persons *vide* personal pronoun, करायाचें होतें remaining the same throughout.

Future, I should be about to make.

Sing.   *Plu.*

m. f. n.   *m. f. n.*

करणार असावा -वी -वें   करणार असावे -व्या -वीं

For 2nd and 3rd persons *vide* असावा (potential), करणार remaining unchanged throughout.

Verbal Noun, करणें the act of doing.

Infinitive, करूं to do.

Participles.

Present, करित, करितां, करितानां doing.

Compound Present, करित असतां being in the state of doing.

Preterite, करून having done.

Compound Past, केलें असतां being in the state of having done.

        m. f. n.

Participial Adjective, केलेला -ली -लें done.
Future, करणार about to do.
Future Passive, करावें fit to be done.

Verbal Noun.

Case.	Sing.	Plu.
Nom.	करणें doing	करणीं
Acc.	करण्यास to do	करण्यांस
Inst.	करण्यानें by doing	करण्यांनीं
Dat.	करण्यास to do	करण्यांस
Abl.	करण्यापासून from doing	करण्यांपासून
Gen.	करण्याचा of doing	करण्यांचा
Loc.	करण्यांत in doing	करण्यांत

Causal Verb.

The causal verb is formed by altering the final णें of the common verb into विणें. (All common verbs, however, cannot be made causal, ex. करविणें to cause to make).

N.B.—करविणें is sometimes written करिवणें, करवणें, करीवणें.

Roots ending in ह and monosyllabic roots take विवणें instead of विणें; ex. लिहणें becomes in its causal form लिहविवणें, and देणें becomes देविवणें. Some intransitive verbs form their causative by changing their root-vowels; ex.,

पड़णें	to fall	पाड़णें	to cause to fall
चरणें	to feed	चारणें	to cause to feed
नरणें	to save	तारणें	to cause to save
टळणें	to pass by	टाळणें	to cause to pass by
नुटणें	to break	तोड़णें	to cause to break
फाटणें	to be rent	फाड़णें	to cause to be rent
फिटणें	to get loose	फेड़णें	to loosen
फुटणें	to get split	फोड़णें	to split
सरणें	to stir	सारणें	to cause to stir
मरणें	to die	मारणें	to kill
दबणें	to subside	दाबणें	to cause to subside

By the addition of an extra व the causative is made doubly causal; ex. करणें to make, करविणें to cause to make, करविवणें to cause to cause to make.

POTENTIAL VERBS.

The potential verb is formed by the addition of ववणें, when the root is monosyllabic, and by the addition of वणें or ववणें when the root is polysyllabic; ex. करवणें to be able to do, जाववणें to be able to go, देववणें to be able to give.

Potential verb, देववणें to be able to give.

61

Tense.	मला or माझ्याने	Indicative Mood.	
Present.		देववतें	It may be given by me.
Present Progressive.	,,	देववत आहे	I can go on giving.
Present Habitual.	,,	देववत असतें	I can be in the habit of giving.
Present Perfect.	,,	देववलें आहे	I have been able to give.
Present Prospective.	,,	देवणार आहे	I may be about to give.
Past.	,,	देववलें	I could give.
Past Progressive.	,,	देववत होतें	I could go on giving.
Past Habitual.	,,	देववें / देववत असे	I could be in the habit of giving.
Pluperfect.	,,	देवलें होतें	I had been able to give.
Complete Perfect.	,,	देववत झालें	I could begin to give.
Past Prospective.	,,	देवणार होतें	I was about to be able to give.
Future.	,,	देववेल	I shall be able to give.
Future Progressive.	,,	देववत असेल	I shall be able to go on giving.
Future Perfect.	,,	देवलें असेल	I shall have been able to give.
Future Prospective.	,,	देवणार असेल	I shall be able to be about to give.

Imperative Mood.

माझ्यानें or मला देववो Let me be able to give.

Subjunctive Mood.

Tense.			
Past.	माझ्यानें or मला देववतें		I should be able to give.
Past Progressive.	,,	,, देववत असतें	I should have been able to be giving.
Pluperfect.	,,	,, देववलें असतें	I should have been able to give.

Potential Mood.

Tense.			
Present.	माझ्यानें or मला देववावें		I may be able to give.
Present Progressive.	,,	,, देववत असावें	I may be able to go on giving.
Present Perfect.	,,	,, देववलें असावें	I may have been able to give.
Past.	,,	,, देववावें होतें / देववायाचें होतें	I might be able to give.
Future.	,,	,, देववणार असावें	I should be about to be able to give.

Verbal Noun.	देववणें	To be able to give.
Infinitive.	देववूं	To be able to give.

Participles.

Present.	देववत, देववतांनां	capable of giving.
Compound Present.	देववत असतां	being in the state of being capable of giving.
Preterite.	देववून	having been capable of giving.
Compound Preterite.	देववलें असतां	being in a state of being able to be given.
	m. *f.* *n.*	
Participial Adjective.	देववलेला-ली-लें	capable of being given.
Future.	देववणार	about to be able to give.
Future Passive.	देववावें	fit to be capable of being given.

VERBAL NOUN.

Case.	Sing.		Plu.
Nom.	देववणें	being capable of giving	देववणीं
Acc.	देववण्यास	to be capable of giving	देववण्यांस
Inst.	देववण्यानें	by being capable of giving	देववण्यांनीं
Dat.	देववण्यास	to be capable of giving	देववण्यांस
Abl.	देववण्यापासून	from being capable of giving	देववण्यांपासून
Gen.	देववण्याचा	of being capable of giving	देववण्यांचा
Loc.	देववण्यांत	in being capable of giving	देववण्यांत

ADVERBS.

Adverbs are indeclinable words used to qualify the meaning of verbs, adjectives, participles, postpositions, and other adverbs; ex.—

Verb.	कुत्रा मोठ्यानें भेंकडतो	The dog barks loudly.
Adjective.	तो फार गर्विष्ठ आहे	He is very proud.
Participle.	तो लवकर चालत आहे	He is going quickly.
Postposition.	तो अगदीं आंत शिरतो	He goes right into.
Adverb.	तो अतिशय मोठ्यानें वाचतो	He reads very loudly.

PARTICLES.

Particles are either postpositions, prepositions, or conjunctions.

POSTPOSITIONS.

Postpositions are indeclinable words used to mark a relation between two words or terms in a sentence; ex. त्याच्या ठायीं in him, तिजजवळ near her.

PREPOSITIONS.

There are in Marâthi a few prepositions which have been borrowed from other languages; ex. अजतरफ from.

CONJUNCTIONS.

Conjunctions are indeclinable words which connect sentences; ex. जर असें करशील तर मार खाशील If you do so you shall eat a beating.

COMPOUND WORDS.

(समास).

In Marâthi there are several words compounded of two or more words of the same or different kinds; ex. आईबाप parents. They may be divided into three classes:—

1. Copulative Compounds (द्वंद्व).

2. Determinative Compounds (including inflexional (तत्पुरुष) and appositional (कर्मधारय).
3. Relative Compounds (बहुव्रीहि).

It must be observed that when a greater or lesser number of words are combined to form one new term, the characteristic signs of case and number are generally rejected by all the members of the compound except the last.

1. COPULATIVE COMPOUNDS.

Compounds of this class consist of nouns which if not compounded would be joined by a particle signifying "and;" ex. ब्रह्माविष्णुमहेश Bramhâ, Vishṇu, Mahesh.

2. DETERMINATIVE COMPOUNDS.

Determinative Compounds consist of two parts, the first of which restricts the signification of the second. They are either inflexional or appositional.

Inflexional Compounds.

When the determinative is used in the sense of a case governed by the second part, the compound is called तत्पुरुष Tutpurusha; ex.—

Acc.	द्विजदण्ड	a Brâhman's punishment.
Inst.	कृपावलोकन	with kind regard.
Dat.	कृष्णार्पण	devoted to Krishṇa.
Abl.	स्वर्गपतन	a fall from heaven.
Gen.	राजवाडा	a king's palace.
Loc.	गृहप्रवेश	entering into a house.

These compounds when attributives take the gender of the noun with which they agree, but when appellatives take generally the gender of the last part of the compound.

Appositional Compounds.

When the determinative (*i. e.* first) part is used in the sense of an apposition expressed by a substantive, adjective, adverb, or particle, the compound is called appositional; नीलगिरी, blue mountain, घनःश्याम as black as a cloud. Compounds of this class may consist of attributives only; ex. शुक्लकृष्ण white and black.

The compounds in which the determinative word is a numeral form a subdivision of this species. Any numeral except *one* may form its first part. It is called द्विगु; ex. चतुर्युग four ages.

मध्यमपदलोपी compounds form a sub-division of this species. शाकपार्थिव is an example of this class of compound.

3. RELATIVE COMPOUNDS.

A determinative compound may be used as the attribute of a substantive, and consequently become an adjective; ex. the karmadharaya compound महाबाहु *great arm* may be used as an attribute of a mighty king in the sense of having a great arm; चक्रपाणि, having a chakra in hand.

VERB CONSTRUCTIONS (PRAYOGAS).

In Marâṭhi there are three systems of construction: (1) *Active* (Kartari), (2) *Passive* (Karmani), (3) *Neuter* (Bhavi).

1. *Active.*—In this construction the verb agrees with its nominative in number, gender, and person; ex. तो पाणी पितो he drinks water.

In this construction the object is generally placed in the nominative case. Proper nouns and pronouns are, however, always put in the accusative case when objects of a verb; ex. तो गोविंदास धरितो he catches Govinda, तो त्याला मारितो he strikes him. Names of animals may optionally be put in the nominative or accusative case; ex. तो घोडा विकतो or तो घोड्यास विकतो he sells a horse.

In poetry the following construction is not uncommon :—

"समयीं पराक्रमातें करिति शुभ यशोधनाश समयज्ञ." मोरोपंत.

2. *Passive.*—In this construction the verb agrees with its object, which is in the nominative case, in number, gender, and person, the agent being generally placed in the instrumental case; ex. मीं घोडा विकला the horse was sold by me.

N.B.—Sentences such as the following, though the agent is not placed in the instrumental case, belong to the passive construction; तुला स्नान करावें लागेल you will have to bathe, आम्हांस रथ करतां येतो we can make (build) a carriage, मला आंबा पाहिजे I want a mango.

The following construction is not uncommon in poetry:—

"वरिलासि मत्सखीनें................." मोरोपंत.

3.—*Neuter.* In this construction the verb is always placed in the neuter gender, third person singular, the subject being generally in the instrumental case, and the object, if the verb is transitive, in the accusative case; ex. मीं तिला धरिलें (lit. it was caught to her by me) I caught her, मीं पलंगावर निजावें (lit. it must be slept on the bed by me) I must sleep on the bed.

N.B.—This construction is only used for animate obects. But the poetical construction—

"पाझांते तोडावें धीरें न कदापि पाप जोडावें"

is not incorrect.

Intransitive verbs in the potential mood follow this or the active construction—

"————बैसावें जे सभेंत मत्तांते." मोरोपंत"

Sentences such as the following, though the agent is not placed in the instrumental case, belong to this construction; ex. मला निजवें लागतें I must sleep, मला जातां येनें I can go, हरीस लिहिलें पाहिजे Hari must write.

Impersonal verbs follow the passive construction; उजाडतें it dawns, सांजावतें it becomes evening.

SYNTAX.

Syntax describes the arrangement of words into sentences, and all syntax may be classified under the heads of Concord and Government.

CONCORDS.

There are in Marâthi two concords :—(1) between the nominative case and the verb; (2) between the adjective &c. and substantive. In Marâthi there is only one government, *i.e.* that of the transitive verb.

1st CONCORD.

Every sentence consists of two parts: the *subject* which is the person or thing spoken of; and the *predicate,* or that which is said of the subject.

The subject of a sentence may be expressed by a substantive or substantival expression; ex. घोडा धांवतो the *horse* runs. त्यानें चोरी केली हें नीट नाहीं *that he should have robbed* is bad.

In Marâthi the subject is in the nominative or the instrumental case; ex. घोडा धांवतो the horse runs, त्यानें चोरी केली he stole.

The verb agrees with its nominative in gender, number, and person; ex. ती स्त्री रडते that woman weeps. When a verb has more than one nominative it agrees with the last; ex. ते आणि ती गेली they and she went. In the case of the imperative mood, if the verb has more than one nominative it agrees with the more worthy; ex. मी व तूं भांवूं let me and you run, तुम्ही व त्या जा let you and them go.

N.B.—In Marâṭhi several nominatives of different genders are sometimes followed by हीं *these*, or अशीं *such*, and the verb takes its gender and number accordingly; ex. मुलगा, मुलगी व मूल हीं आलीं a boy, a girl, and a child—*these* came.

The predicate consists either of a verb or of a noun (adjective or substantive) joined to the subject by the substantive verb असणें to be. When the predicate is a verb, it agrees with its subject in gender, number, and person; ex. ती निजते she sleeps.

When the predicate consists of an adjective or a participial adjective, it agrees with its subject in gender, number, and case; ex. तरवार चांगली आहे the sword is good, घोडा धरलेला आहे the horse has been caught.

When the predicate consists of a substantive, it cannot, as a rule, agree with the subject either in gender or number; ex. रामा मूल आहे Râmâ is a child.

When one noun is used to explain another, it is put in the same case as the noun it explains; ती बाई लक्ष्मी आहे that woman is a Lakshmî.

The Nominative Case.

The nominative is the case which *names* the subject of a proposition, *i. e.* the person or thing of which anything is predicated.

N.B.—The subject in Marâthi may be either in the nominative or the instrumental case.

In Marâthi the use of the nominative for the accusative case is common; ex. तो वाघ मारतो he kills a tiger.

In Marâthi the use of the nominative for the genitive case is also common; ex. तीन तोळे सोनें three tolahs of gold.

The Accusative Case.

The accusative denotes the object of transitive verbs.

Verbs and adjectives denoting extent of time or space govern the accusative of the noun describing that extent; ex. तो तीन कोश चालला he walked three *koss*, नदी तीन कोश लांब आहे the river is three *koss* long.

The Instrumental Case.

The instrumental case denotes the agent, implement, or the means by which anything is done. It also expresses the manner or degree in which any object is effected, and also the characteristics by which any object is marked; तो मोठ्यानें बोलतो he talks loudly, तो शेंडीनें ब्राह्मण दिसतो he seems to be a Brâhman by his lock of hair.

The Dative Case.

The dative generally expresses the person or thing to or for which, or in regard to which, something is, or is done: it may therefore be termed the case of the remoter object.

In Marâthi the dative sometimes stands for the locative case; ex. डोक्यास त्याच्या पागोटें होतें a puggree was on his head, तो बेळगांवास गेला he went to Belgaum

The dative is optionally used with the gerundive for the instrumental case; ex. तें मला करायाचें आहे I have to do that. The dative is also used in Marâṭhi wherein other languages the accusative (and in Sanscrit the ablative) is used; ex. मी त्याला भितों I fear him.

The Ablative Case.

The ablative expresses a variety of relations defining and modifying the predicate—that is, all those relations which in English are expressed by the preposition *from*; ex. बेळगांवाहून तो गेला he went from Belgaum, मत्सरापासून द्वेष होतो hatred springs from envy, बेळगांवाहून गोंवें तीस कोश आहे Goa is thirty *koss* from Belgaum.

The Genitive Case.

The genitive serves principally to denote that relation between two substantives by which the two conjointly express only one idea, the genitive supplying the place of a qualifying adjective.

In Marâṭhi the genitive is sometimes used for the locative case; ex. तो रात्रीचा वाचितो he reads at night: and also for the instrumental; ex. माझ्या बोलण्याचा त्याला राग येतो he becomes angry at my words: and also for the ablative; ex. मी कालचा त्यास सांगतों I have been telling him since yesterday.

The subjective genitive is common in Marâṭhi; ex. लोकांचा जुलूम the tyranny exercised by the people: the objective genitive is uncommon; ex. ईश्वराची भक्ति God's worship.

The Locative Case.

The locative case denotes the place where, and the time at which anything is or is done.

In Marāṭhi the locative is sometimes used for the instrumental case; ex. रिकाम्या हातीं बाजारांत जाऊं नये one should not go to the market empty-handed, तोंडें तो बोलला he answered verbally. This case is also used sometimes where the preposition वर *on* might be expected to govern its noun; ex. पायांत जोडा a shoe on a foot, बोटांत अंगठी a ring on a finger.

The Vocative Case.

The vocative case is used to address a person or thing, and is inserted in clauses without affecting their construction.

2ND CONCORD.

The adjective, pronoun, numeral or participle used attributively agrees with its substantive (to a certain extent) in gender, number, and case.

N.B.—It seems certain that in Marāṭhi adjectives formerly had case-terminations, as they have in Sanscrit. These terminations have been dropped, but we have the base form of the adjective to agree with its substantive when in any case other than the nominative; ex. चांगल्या पुरुषांचा of a good man.

The same rule applies to pronouns and particles used attributively; ex. त्या स्त्रियेचा of that woman, भरलेल्या तरवारीनें with a sword taken hold of.

Numerals ending in अ (exc. एक्, which in cases other than the nominative becomes एका) do not take their base form when qualifying substantives.

When there are several substantives of the same gender, the adjective agreeing with them is made plural, and of the same gender as the substantives.

It is usual to introduce हा *this* or असा *such* after the substantives with whose gender and number they agree; ex. त्या स्त्रिया व मुली या चांगल्या आहेत those women and girls, *these* are good.

When there are many substantives of different genders, the adjective agreeing with them is put in the neuter plural, हीं or अशीं being generally added before the adjective, as in the foregoing rule; ex. मुलगा, मुलगी, व मुलगें हीं चांगलीं आहेत, the boy, girl, and child, *these* are good.

The Relative (Definitive) Pronoun.

In Marâthi the (so-called) relative pronoun is seldom used as it is in other languages. In Marâthi it precedes its substantive, with which it agrees in gender, number, and case, just as adjectives do, being followed by a demonstrative pronoun; ex. जो पुरुष तेथें धांवत आहे त्याला बोलाव call that man who is running there.

It is also used independently; ex. जो श्रम करितो तो उद्योगी he is industrious who labours.

Government or Dependence.

When one word depends upon another it is governed by it. In Marâthi the only example of government is that between a transitive verb and accusative case; ex. मी त्याला मारितों I strike him.

N.B.—This is *objective combination*, which must be distinguished from *attributive combination*, which is that of the substantive and adjective &c., and also from *predicative combination*, which is that of the subject and predicate.

CLAUSES AND THEIR RELATIONS TO ONE ANOTHER.

A clause is either independent or subordinate. Independent clauses simply state facts in the form of assertions or questions. Subordinate sentences are generally so constructed as to be unable to stand alone, and they can only be understood when viewed in connection with another. Subordinate clauses are joined to their leading clauses by conjunctions; ex. तो वाईट आहे म्हणून मला आवडत नाहीं he is bad, therefore I do not like him: by relative pronouns; ex. जे जे तेथें होते त्यांस हें माहित आहें all those who were there know this: by demonstrative pronouns; ex. मी काय करूं असें तो विचारूं लागला he began to ask what he should do.

Two or more clauses may be joined together in such a way, by copulative or adversative conjunctions, that none of them is subordinate to another. Such clauses are co-ordinate, and they may be all leading or all subordinate clauses of the same sentence.

PARTICIPLES.

Those participles, which are declinable, are like adjectives, in that they agree with their substantives in gender, number, and case. Participles can govern cases; ex. त्याला मारून तो पळाला having struck him he ran off. The future and past participles agree with their substantives; ex. धांवणारा घोडा the horse about to run; बांधली गाय the tied-up cow.

The indefinite past (preterite) participle is used to suspend clauses, and takes the place of conjunctions; ex. तिला पाहून तो गेला having seen her he went. In Marâthî this participle can be used absolutely; ex. पक्ष्यांनीं निश्चय

कहून त्यास ठार मारिलें the birds, having determined, slew him. The present participle is also used absolutely; ex. दिवस स्वच्छ असतां लोक फिरतात the day being fine, people walk about.

PROSODY.

All Marâthi verse is made up of long or short syllables. A short letter is made long by the lengthening of its vowel; ex. क is short, का is long : इ is short, ई is long : कि is short, की is long.

A short letter becomes long when it precedes a complex consonant, an anusvâra, or a visarga. It may be made long if occurring at the end of a line.

There are only two kinds of feet, trisyllabic and quadrisyllabic. The following list shows the trisyllabic feet:—

1.	Nagana	∪	∪	∪
2.	Magana	—	—	—
3.	Jagana	∪	—	∪
4.	Ragana	—	∪	—
5.	Bhagana	—	∪	∪
6.	Sagana	∪	∪	—
7.	Jagana	∪	—	—
8.	Tagan	—	—	∪

Of the trisyllabic feet metre there are twenty-one orders, which are again divided into numerous varieties. This metre is regulated by the "number of syllables," irrespective of their quantity. Stanzas or Shlokas generally consist of two lines or hemistichs, each of which is again divided into two parts, so that the entire Shloka is composed of four lines. These lines are generally, but not always, of equal length and corresponding quantities. The following are the different orders of this metre, with their varieties:—

1. *Gayatri*, containing 6 s. (syllables) in each of its four lines, and having 11 v. (varieties). It is uncommon.
2. *Ushnih*, 7 s. 8 v. (uncommon).
3. *Anushtubh*, 8 s. 12 v.; ex.:

निर्य नव्हे त्या करितां कां झटतां कां श्रमतां ।
जा भगवन्नाम वदा निर्भय गा त्यास सदा ॥

This variety is called माणवक.

4. *Vrihati*, 9 s. 12 v. (uncommon).
5. *Pankti*, 10 s. 14 v. (uncommon).
6. *Trishtubh*, 11 s. 4 v; ex.:

वामअंकगतभूमिकुमारी वामबाहुसुरता सुकुमारी ।
वल्कलांबरजटाअभिराम देखतो भरत त्या अभिराम ॥

7. *Jagati*, 12 s. 30 v.; ex.:

नसे गर्व अंगीं सदा वीतरागी
क्षमा शांति भोगी दयादक्षयोगी ।
नसे लोभ ना क्षोभ ना दैन्यवाणा
अशा लक्षणीं जाणिजे योगिराणा ॥

8. *Atijagati*, 13 s. 16 v.
9. *Shakkari*, 14 s. 20 v.; ex.:

तूं ईश ये रिति उपाधि जयासि विद्या
तूं जीवही धरनि ही अससी अविद्या ।
जो स्वानुभूत रहित त्रिगुणाभिमान
त्यातें नमो स्थिरचरांतहि जो समान ॥

10. *Atishakvari*, 15 s. 18 v.; ex.:

करि हरि यमुनाहो मूद गंगावनाची
मिरवि धवल पुर्यां दीप्ति गंगावनाची ।
सित असित नद्यांच्या संगमीं श्रीत्रिवेणी
तसिच यदुपतीनें घातली चित्रवेणी ॥

11. *Ashti*, 16 s. 12 v. (uncommon).
12. *Atyashti*, 17 s. 17 v.; ex.:

॥ पृथ्वी ॥

कडया वरुनियां उडयां प्रथम टाकुनी च्या गडयां
गडे पशुप भेटती तटतटां मुर्जी आंगडया ।
फुगोनि तनु फार ती मनगटीं कडीं दाटती
सुखें अमित वाटती विरहसिंधुतें आटती ॥

शिखरिणी·

असा येतां देखे रथानिकट तो श्यामल हरी
नृपा गांगेयाच्या हृदयें भरल्या प्रेमलहरी ।
शरांतें चापांतें त्यजुनि वदला गद्गदरवें
जगन्नाथें केलें मज सकल लोकांत बरवें ॥

मन्दाक्रान्ता·

नानाशास्त्रान्वित तनय हा मैथिलेचा प्रतापी
आविर्भावें दहन करितो पण्डितांच्या हि पंक्ती
ऐसा च्याचा भुज बळ नव्हे स्तोम ज्ञानामृताचा
घाला घाली तुडवि विपदीं कीर्तिभ्रष्टां समस्तां ॥

हरिणी.

प्रथम गमला ऐसा मोठा अधर्मचि तो दिलें
नमन वचना कामें नाहीं च तें अनुमोदिलें ।

मग कथित या जाया जाया स्वसंशय वृत्त मीं
रति मदन तूं हें तें होय प्रभा स्मर हृत्तमीं ॥

13. *Dhriti*, 18 s. 17 v. (uncommon).
14. *Atidhriti*, 19 s. 13 v.; ex. :

शार्दूलविक्रीडित.

छायानायकसा निदाघसमयीं छाया करी तो विधू ।
वांया या हृदयाश्रमासि करितो दायादसा हा मधू
जाया जे रुचली मनीं तिजकडे जायानयें कीं पहा
रायाला न गमे न जाय रजनी आयास होती महा ॥

15. *Kriti*, 20 s. 4 v. (uncommon).
16. *Prakriti*, 21 s. 3 v.; ex. :

स्रग्धरा.

भृंगांची पंक्ति मौर्वी कुसुममयधनू बाण तेहि प्रसूनें
लीलेने दास केले असुर सुरनर मौढ ही ब्रह्मसूनें ।
तोचि प्रद्युम्न साक्षात् अजितसुत युवा ज्या रणीं शस्त्रपाणी
बाहे पाहे तदर्वीं तिलसहित तया सोडिजे कां न पाणी.

17. *Akriti*, 22 s. 3 v. (uncommon).
18. *Vikriti*, 23 s. 6 v. (uncommon).
19. *Sankriti*, 24 s. 5 v. (uncommon).
20. *Atikriti*, 25 s. 2 v. (uncommon).
21. *Utkriti*, 26 s. 3 v. (uncommon).

Of the quadrisyllabic feet metre there are sixteen orders, each of which is again divided into sixteen varieties. Five of these orders are important. This metre is regulated by the quantity of syllables.

1. *Arya*, contains 30 syllables in the first line and 27 in the second. Each stanza contains two lines, and each line seven and a half feet. The

sixth foot of the second line consists of a short syllable only. In the first line the sixth foot must be a long syllable between two short or four short syllables. The odd feet in either line must never be a long syllable between two short; ex.:

नूतनपल्लव फुटला असला तर आणला प्रियेनें तो ।
लवकर चाखायाला तोंडाशीं गज पहा नेतो ॥

2. *Udgiti*, contains 27 syllables in the first line and 30 in the second.

3. *Upagiti*, contains 27 syllables in each line; ex.:

हें सर्व अंग फुललें कुमुद जसें चंद्रकिरणांनीं ।
फुलतें काय कधीं तें सांग वरें सूर्यकिरणांनीं ॥

4. *Giti*, contains 30 short syllables in each line; ex.:

ह्मणऊनि अनुसरावें सुज्ञें न क्रोधलोभकाममता ।
पतनार्थ कां अहंता पोषावी गा तशीच कां ममता ॥

5. *Aryagiti*, contains 32 short syllables in each line; ex.:

काढित असतां धारा, टाकुनि अनुसरति युवति जगदाधारा ।
तापविता दुध मणिकीं, त्यजिति अमृत पाजितो विबुधमणिकीं ॥

Besides the metres given above, which are all derived from Sanscrit, there are some few purely Marâthi, viz., Pada, Ovi, Abhang, Dindi, Saki, Savayi, Lavani, Katava, Arti, Bhupali. There are varieties of these too numerous to be mentioned here.

APPENDIX I.

GRAMMATICAL TERMS.

Letter	अक्षर
Vowel	स्वर
Short	ह्रस्व
Long	दीर्घ
Consonant	व्यंजन
Combination Letters	संधि
Elision	लोप
Insertion	आगम
Change	आदेश
{ Uninflected Word { Crude Word	प्रकृति
Base Form	सामान्यरूप
Inflected Word	पद
Affix	प्रत्यय
Prefix	उपसर्ग
Sentence	वाक्य
Noun	नाम
Gender	लिंग
Masculine	पुल्लिंग
Feminine	स्त्रीलिंग
Neuter	नपुंसकलिंग
Number	वचन
Singular	एकवचन
Plural	अनेकवचन

Case		विभक्ति
	Nominative (1st)	प्रथमा
	Accusative (2nd)	द्वितीया
	Instrumental (3rd)	तृतीया
	Dative (4th)	चतुर्थी
	Ablative (5th)	पंचमी
	Genitive (6th)	षष्ठी
	Locative (7th)	सप्तमी
	Vocative (8th)	संबोधन
Declension		रूप
Adjective		विशेषण
Numeral		संख्यावाचक
Pronoun		सर्वनाम
Verb		क्रियापद
Root		धातु
Agent (nom. to verb)		कर्ता
Object (governed by verb)		कर्म
Person		पुरुष
	1st	प्रथम
	2nd	द्वितीय
	3rd	तृतीय
Inflected Forms of the Verb		आख्यातरूप
Mood		अर्थ
	Indicative	स्वार्थ
	Imperative	आज्ञार्थ
	Subjunctive	संकेतार्थ
	Potential	विध्यर्थ
	Verbal Noun	धातुसाधिननाम
{ Participle } { Gerund }		धातुसाधिन

Tense	काल
Present	वर्त्तमान
Present Progressive	अपूर्ण वर्त्तमान
Present Habitual	रीति वर्त्तमान
Present Perfect	भूत वर्त्तमान
Present Prospective	भविष्य वर्त्तमान
Past (Preterite)	भूत
Past Progressive	अपूर्ण भून
Past Habitual	रीति भून
Pluperfect	भूत भून
Complete Perfect	पूर्ण भूत
Past Prospective	भविष्य भून
Future	भविष्य
Future Progressive	अपूर्ण भविष्य
Future Perfect	वर्त्तमान भविष्य
Future Prospective	भविष्य भविष्य
Active Verb	सकर्मक क्रियापद
Neuter Verb	अकर्मक क्रियापद
Passive Verb	कर्म कर्त्तरि क्रियापद
Verbal Construction	प्रयोग
Active	कर्त्तरि
Passive	कर्मणि
Neuter	भावी
Causal Verb	प्रयोज्य क्रियापद
Potential Verb	शक्य क्रियापद
Adverb	क्रियाविशेषण अव्यय
Particles	अव्यय
Postposition	शब्दयोगी अव्यय
(Preposition)	(उपसर्ग)

Conjunction	उभयान्वयी अव्यय
Interjection	उद्गारवाचक
Compound Noun	समास
Syntax	वाक्यरचना
Prosody	कवितालक्षण

APPENDIX II.

EXERCISES IN PARSING, GRAMMAR, AND READING.

PARSING.

1. खोतजी गेल्यानंतर तिणें भावांच्या तोंडांवर त्यांणीं खोताचा अपमान केला तो बापास सांगितला.

खोतजी	Common noun, 1st decl., sing. num., mas. gend., nom. case, subj. to गेला.
गेला	(गेल्यानंतर=गेला या नंतर) Intr. verb, past tense, indic. mood, 3rd pers. sing., mas. gend., agreeing with its subj. खोतजी. This is the active construction.
या	Base form of हा, demons. pron., neut. gend., sing. num., governed by the postpos. नंतर.
नंतर	Postpos. governing या.
तिणें	Personal pron., fem. gend., sing. num., inst. case (from ती), joined with सांगितला.
भावांच्या	Com. noun, mas. gend., plu. num., base form (modified gen.), governed by तोंडां.
तोंडां	Com. noun, neut. gend., plu. num., base form, governed by वर.

वर	Postpos. governing तोंडां.
त्यांनीं	Pers. pron., mas. gend., plu. num., inst. case (from तो), joined with केला.
न्वोनाचा	Com. noun, mas. gend., sing. num., gen. case, dependent on अपमान.
अपमान	Com. noun, mas. gend., sing. num., nom. case, subj. to केला.
केला	Trans. verb, past tense, sing. num., mas. gend., agreeing with अपमान. This is the passive construction.
तो	Demons. pron., mas. gen., sing. num., nom. case, subj. to सांगितला.
बापास	Com. noun, sing. num., mas. gend., dat. case, governed by सांगितला.
सांगितला	Trans. verb, indic. mood, 3rd pers., sing. num., past tense, mas. gend., agreeing with its subject तो. This is the passive construction.

II. (a) मी घोड्याला मारितों.

मी	Pers. pron., mas. gend., sing. num., nom. case, subject to मारितों.
घोड्याला	Com. noun, mas. gend., sing. num., acc. case, object to मारितों.
मारितों	Trans. verb, indic. mood, pres. tense, 1st pers., sing. num., mas. gend., agreeing with its subject मी. This is the active construction with a transitive verb.

(b) तो धांवतो.

तो   Pers. pron., sing. num., mas. gend., nom. case, subject to धांवतो.

धांवतो   Intrans. verb., indic. mood, 3rd pers., sing. num., mas. gend., pres. tense, agreeing with its subject तो. This is the active construction with an intransitive verb.

III. मला निजावें लागतें.

मला   Pers. pron., sing. num., masc. gend., dat. case, depending on निजावें.

निजावें.   Fut. pass. part., neut. gend., sing. num., dependent on लागतें. The root is निज.

लागतें   Intrans. verb, 3rd pers., sing. num., neut. gend., pres. tense, indic. mood; the root is लाग. This is the neuter construction.

GRAMMAR.

VERBAL AFFIXES.

The following terminations for the most part express *action, doer, condition, nature, capability, doing.*

Term.	Ex.		Term.	Ex.	
अ.	हेर	a spy.	आ.	लंगडा	a limper.
आळ.	लाजाळू	bashful.	ऊ.	पोटभरू	a gorger.
आऊ.	विकाऊ	fit to be sold.	णाऊ	ठेवणाऊ	fit to be kept.
ईक.	खर्चीक	a spendthrift.	का.	मारका	a beater.

Term.	Ex.		Term.	Ex.	
रा.	लाजरा	a bashful person.	यार.	विक्या	a seller.
ईव.	जाणीव	a wise person.	ईत.	चकचकीत	a shining.

The following express *completion* of that which the root expresses:—

Term.	Ex.		Term.	Ex.	
ईव.	पाळींव	tamed.	ईत.	पडीत	fallow.
ईर.	फुटीर	fit to be broken.	ईल.	छापील	printed.
ट.	कुजट	rotten.	ईक.	पढीक	instructed.

The following express *state, condition, act*:—

Term.	Ex.		Term.	Ex.	
अवा.	बोलवा	rumour.	आट.	गडगडाट	thunder.
ई.	उडी	a leap.	ण.	चढण	an ascent.
णा.	करुणा	pity.	णी.	करणी	a doing.
णूक.	वर्तणूक	conduct.	वण.	वाढवण	increasing.
ऊ.	खाऊ	sweetmeat.	ऊं.	हसूं	derision.

ADJECTIVAL AFFIXES.

The following terminations when applied to adjectives form abstract nouns:—

आ.	ताठा	haughtiness.	आई.	भिटाई	boldness.
ई.	गरिबी	poverty.	पण.	वेडेपण	madness.
			पणा.	थोरपणा	greatness.
गिरी.	कामगिरी	work.	की.	माणूसकी	humanity.
वा.	गारवा	coolness.	ता.	गृहस्थता	gentility.
वी.	थोरवी	greatness.	न्य.	दानृन्य	generosity.
वाणा.	दीनवाणा	pitiableness.			

NOMINAL AFFIXES.

Term.	Ex.		Term.	Ex.	
कुली.	धनुकुली	a small bow.	कट.	वळकट	strong.
रूं.	पाखरूं	a bird.	आर.	कुंभार	a potter.
कार.	ग्रंथकार	an author.	आडी.	सोंगाडी	a hypocrite.
आरी.	पिंजारी	a carder.	आळू.	झोंपाळू	a sleepy person.
आळ.	हाताळ	a thief.	वट.	रानवट	barbarous.
वटा.	गारवटा	cold.	कर.	खेळकर	a player.
			करी.	भाडेकरी	a letter of carts.
मंत.	श्रीमंत	rich.	चा.	हातचा	manual.

PREFIXES.

Pref.	Meaning.	Ex.	
अभि.	to.	अधिकार	authority.
अभि.	on both sides.	अभ्यास	study.
उत्.	out.	उत्तेजन	encouragement.
दुर्.	bad.	दुर्दैव	misfortune.
प्रति.	against.	प्रतिशब्द	echo.
इति.	in this way.	इतिहास	history.
अप.	away from.	अपमान	dishonour.
अव.	away from.	अवकृपा	disfavour.
उप.	near to.	उपकार	benefaction.
निर्.	out of.	निर्गुण	without qualities.
सम्.	together.	संबंध	connection.
कु.	bad.	कुकर्म	bad action.
भिक्.	reproach.	भिक्कार	hooting.
प्रातः	early.	प्रातःकाळ	morning.

Pref.	Meaning.	Ex.	
स.	} with.	सजीव	living.
सह.		सहवास	living with.
न.	not.	नास्तिक	infidel.
बहि:.	outward.	बहिष्कार	excommunication.
स्वयम्	self.	स्वयंभू	self-born.

तें तूं म्हटलेंस. Why is this wrong?

There is here a confusing of two verbal constructions. म्हटलें is correct.

The following verbs can take the active construction when other verbs require the passive :—

जेवणें	to dine.	चावणें	to bite.
बोलणें	to speak.	पावणें	to obtain.
विणें	to bring forth.	विसरेंण	to forget.
आचरणें	to practise.	हरणें	to carry away.
पांघरणें	to clothe.	पिणें	to drink.
लेणें	to put on.	म्हणणें	to say.
समजणें	to understand.	न्हाणें	to bathe.
पढणें	to study.	नेसणें	to put on.
भिणें	to fear.	लागणें	to touch.
शिकणें	to learn.	शिवणें	to touch.

The terminations ता and त्व are equivalent in every respect excepting gender, and the fact of त्व being more ornate than ता. The student will find that Molesworth contradicts himself with regard to this subject: *vide* Molesworth's Dict., pp. vi. and 393. Thus प्रभुता comes from the *noun* प्रभु, and not from an adjective, and its signification is *the office of a lord*.

The termination पण is properly only applied to Marâṭhi nouns. Nouns ending in पणा are inflected in the same way as those ending in पण, with which they are identical, excepting in gender.

In Marâṭhi the *augment* आगम is found. It exists in व्हावा, where व is an augment, and in करित, where इ is an augment.

The *substitution of letters for letters of the root* आदेश is common :—

Ex. मुख + इंदु become मुखेंदु moon-faced; सोसणें becomes सोशित, where श is the substituted letter.

Reduplication, वैनःपुन्य, is sometimes found as in the word झाला, which coming from होणें was originally जहाला.

READING.

पत्रावरून मला असें दिसलें कीं तों त्या दोन्ही
Pattrâwarûna malâ asen disalen kîn to tyâ donhî
गोष्टींस कबूल झाला वासुदेवास मात्र तें खरें
goshṭînsa kabûla zâlâ Vâsudevâsa mâtra ten kharen
वाटलें नाहीं. माझ्या मामा तूं कठोर होऊं नको.
vâṭalen nâhîn. Mâzyâ mâmâ tûn kaṭhora houn nako.
बरें तर पाहूं या.
Baren tara pâhûn yâ.

साकी.

देवा अहें मंदमती मी नकळे मजला काहीं
Devâ ahen mandamatî mî nakalle majalâ kânhîn
अज्ञानजलीं भ्रमतों श्रमतों बहुविध मी
ajnyânajalîn bhramaton shramaton bahuvidha mî
शंकाहीं.
shankânhîn.

ERRATA.

Page	Line	For	Read
4	13	ow	ou
4	13	वन	वन
6	13	वली	वलि
7	last	इं	इुं
9	last	चाकू	चाकू
17	21	जमहून	मजहून
51	25	(ण)	(नं)
54	2	करता	करिता
59	14	causal	causal)
59	15	make).	make
66	last but one	nominative	subject
67	last but four	subject	agent
68	12	passive	neuter

BOMBAY:
PRINTED AT THE EDUCATION SOCIETY'S PRESS, BYCULLA.